# What People Are Saying about *Never Alone*

"Dottie and I have attended the Ferguson marriage seminars and have grown tremendously from the perspective we gained. This one-of-a-kind marriage book offers a paradigm-shifting truth: God wants to meet our needs for aloneness, and he wants to involve you as his partner in meeting your spouse's needs through the power of his Spirit. In this theocentric model for marriage, the question is not so much what *you* get out of your marriage but what *God* gets out of your marriage. Discover that answer, and you'll discover a deepened, more intimate relationship with your spouse." **Josh McDowell,** founder, Josh McDowell Ministry

"David and Teresa have done it again! In *Never Alone* the Fergusons connect with the core needs of couples. Not only do they ask the right questions, but their answers hit the target. These practical principles are rooted in the Scriptures, compellingly illustrated, and anchored by the credibility of the Fergusons and their years of fruitful ministry. This book will transform a 'not so good' marriage into a 'very good' marriage. Thank you, David and Teresa, for putting your heart on paper. You have given us a treasure, an enduring gift!" **Dr. Crawford W. Loritts Jr.,** associate U.S. director, Campus Crusade for Christ

"What the authors refer to as 'the mystery of marriage' is beautifully unscrambled in this book. Focusing on the three-dimensional nature of marriage—a husband, a wife, and Christ—this intriguing, practical, and very helpful book is essential reading for all married couples." **Dr. D. James Kennedy,** senior minister, Coral Ridge Presbyterian Church

"The Fergusons have once again provided biblical hope and practical help for couples. This book addresses the need of intimacy with clarity and authority." **Dennis Rainey,** executive director, FamilyLife

"It is easy to slide into marital boredom and dissatisfaction. All you have to do is nothing. Go through the motions. Settle for routine without the vitality of intimacy. No spark. Together, but very alone. David and Teresa Ferguson have discovered that there *is* more! And, in this book, they open the door to a marriage that blossoms with the freshness that God intended. The truths you will learn can change your life by revolutionizing your marriage. The Fergusons are gifted with insight and compassion. You will be enriched by this book. You owe it to your spouse and your marriage to give these truths priority. It will be a delightful, new beginning." **Randall A. Bach,** superintendent, Eastern Region Open Bible Churches

"David and Teresa Ferguson have nailed the heart of a strong and successful marriage in *Never Alone*. As we become colleagues with Christ in *his* purposes in our spouse's life, we can be close to each other as husband and wife, meet each other's intimate needs, and face the challenges and difficulties of life victoriously. Pastors and counselors should give a copy of *Never*

*Alone* as a marriage guidebook to each couple they counsel." **Dr. Dal Shealy,** president/CEO, Fellowship of Christian Athletes

"This book is a must for all married couples. Woven through this personal account of David and Teresa's journey, from a marriage on the brink of collapse to its transformation to fulfillment and intimacy, is a radically new understanding about the whole purpose and experience of marriage. Focusing on God's intention for marriage, the Fergusons open up an opportunity to experience a depth of love that many married couples have not thought was possible." **Alister Mort,** vicar, St. Mark's Church, Leamington Spa, Warwickshire, England

"I am amazed once again at the freshly anointed insight of David and Teresa Ferguson. In *Never Alone* they uncover treasures of marriage wisdom that have long lain hidden beneath the debris generated by modern society's ceaseless attack on God's primary institution. The Fergusons' transparency in sharing their own struggles is a refreshing contrast to the attempts of other writers who often make their lives appear picture-perfect. These are real people with real problems who have found real marital redemption by bringing God into the midst of their relationship. David and Teresa have a unique way of helping their readers experience God's Word as a part of life rather than merely studying it as an academic exercise. I heartily recommend this work to couples anticipating marriage, those newly married, and those who have been married for many years. All will find hope and help on these pages." **Larry Duncan,** director of family ministries, Church of God of Prophecy

"David and Teresa Ferguson bring enthusiasm and excitement to the topic of marriage. Through this captivating book the Fergusons openly share their failures and joy in marriage and give couples valuable insights, scriptural direction, and sound advice. Their style is refreshing and filled with their desire to minister to marriages and families. What impresses us most about David and Teresa is their giving of themselves through ministry to one of the most important issues to our world—strong and healthy marriages." **Lee and Jan Kremer,** U.S. national leadership, Worldwide Marriage Encounter

"Again David and Teresa Ferguson have clearly championed and clarified what Great Commandment love looks like, how it acts, and how to see lives changed through experiencing that love in lives, marriages, and churches. Filled with biblically intense material, this book clearly presents skills needed to experience Great Commandment love in your marriage. I highly commend this resource." **Dr. Dann Spader,** executive director, Sonlife Ministries

"In *Never Alone*, David and Teresa Ferguson once again demonstrate their remarkable insights into the dynamics of the marriage relationship. They are especially good at pinpointing the "hurts" that harm a marriage, but their practical yet powerful approaches to healing those hurts are what make this book so valuable. *Never Alone* is not a rehash of old methodologies; it is a fresh, scriptural perspective on what makes good marriages work. I highly recommend it." **Dr. Robert Fisher,** director, Center for Spiritual Renewal

# NEVER
## alone

*David & Teresa Ferguson*

TYNDALE HOUSE PUBLISHERS, INC. WHEATON, ILLINOIS

Visit Tyndale's exciting Web site at www.tyndale.com

*Never Alone*

Copyright © 2001 by Intimate Life Ministries. All rights reserved.

Cover photograph copyright © 2000 by LWA/Dann Tardif/The Stock Market Photo Agency. All rights reserved.

Designed by Timothy R. Botts with Luke Daab

Edited by Lynn Vanderzalm

**Library of Congress Cataloging-in-Publication Data**

Ferguson, David, date
  Never alone / David and Teresa Ferguson.
    p. cm.
  ISBN 0-8423-3482-3
  1. Marriage—Religious aspects—Christianity.   I. Ferguson, Teresa, date II. Title

BV835 .F47 2000
248.8′44—dc21                                                    00-061984

Printed in the United States of America

05  04  03  02  01
8   7   6   5   4   3   2   1

# CONTENTS

# Acknowledgments

There was a time that I questioned whether the mystery of marriage could to any degree be successfully written in a book. It couldn't have been done without the extraordinary contributions and collaborative efforts of a number of talented and ministry-focused people. I would like to thank the following people for their involvement in this process. Thank you.

To my wife, Teresa, who has "journeyed" with me in this union called marriage. She has endured the lean years and experienced the blessings of discovering what God wants to get out of our marriage. Without Teresa's having experienced the truth of God's Word in our marriage, this book would never have been written.

To my children and their spouses, who are in ministry with Teresa and me.

To the Intimate Life team for their constant support, nurture, and encouragement; and to the growing network of Great Commandment churches and trainers who have ministered to countless married couples and who have been the source of so many illustrations in this book.

To Dave Bellis, who helped me overcome my reluctance to commit so many elements of this marriage message to writing, who labored with me to incorporate biblical principles from our meetings together, and who fleshed out the structure of the book and completed the written draft of the manuscript.

To Ed Stewart, whose writing skills took the written draft to a new level of amplification and clarity that is both inspiring and challenging to the reader.

To Lynn Vanderzalm, who has become more than our Tyndale House editor. Lynn's insights, wise counsel, and editorial skills have provided direction in guiding the manuscript to a clearer and sharper focus.

Finally, to Ron Beers and Ken Petersen of Tyndale House for their courage to stay the course and for their vision not only to see this project through but also to help perpetuate Great Commandment marriages throughout this country and around the world.

*David Ferguson*

# How God Can Get
# the Most out of Your Marriage

I t had been another stressful yet fulfilling day of juggling a secular job and a demanding ministry to students. My schedule had been packed with typical activities: an early morning discipleship group, a number of appointments at the office where I worked, lunch with a church elder, several phone calls from students, and another round of tinkering with a faulty computer program. I left a pile of work on my desk at six o'clock to run home for a quick supper. Then I hurried off to the church for a counseling appointment and a committee meeting that would last until past ten.

As usual, my wife, Teresa, and the children barely noticed that I had come and gone at suppertime. They were accustomed to my brief appearances and quick disappearances at the house. But I prided myself in being diligent in both my secular work and my part-time ministry, as evidenced by the long hours I put in.

By the time I got home late that night, Teresa was in bed but still awake. I slipped into bed beside her and turned out the light. We talked in generalities about the day. I described my accomplishments, and she related how the kids had behaved—and misbehaved—at home.

At this point in our marriage, our conversations were rather superficial, as was the rest of our relationship. I was so busy with my job and leading a growing student ministry, and she was so busy running the home that we rarely connected deeply with each other.

We were not enemies, yet our marriage had a distance that was unsettling to me.

Staring up at the ceiling in the darkness, I addressed the issue. "Teresa, I sense a dryness between us, like we live on opposite sides of a big desert. We are so involved in our own separate worlds of activity that we hardly notice each other. Is this the way it's always going to be with us?"

There was silence on Teresa's side of the bed, followed by a deep sigh. "I don't know, David."

*W*

*E were not enemies, yet our marriage had a distance that was unsettling to me.*

Finally I found the courage to ask the question that had been haunting me for months. "Teresa, do you really love me?"

Silence again. When Teresa finally answered, I was not prepared for the directness of her response. "David, I don't feel anything for you. I'm just numb."

The words stung my heart. I didn't know what to say. I knew there was some distance between us, but she was talking about a complete lack of love.

Keep in mind that both Teresa and I were deeply involved in Christian leadership at the time. We provided premarital and marital counseling in our church. We would soon be teaching together at retreats and conferences on biblical principles for a strong marriage. We were supposed to know what makes a marriage work. Our relationship wasn't perfect, but up until that night I had thought it was working all right. But Teresa's shocking answer suddenly caused me to wonder if we had any future together at all.

## SOMETHING VITAL WAS MISSING FROM OUR MARRIAGE

That sobering exchange in our bedroom took place more than twenty years ago. It was the beginning of an intense, sometimes painful, and ultimately fulfilling marital journey for me and

2

Teresa—a journey that continues to this day. Part of what you will read in the chapters ahead reveals how a marriage—even a relatively good marriage—can arrive at the point where one or both partners might say to the other something like, "I don't feel anything for you. I'm just numb." But most of what you will read focuses on how God rekindled our love and transformed our marriage—and thousands of others like ours—into a relationship of increasing joy, fulfillment, and blessing.

Your marriage may or may not have deteriorated to the point ours had those many years ago. Perhaps you have a wonderful marriage. If so, you know the importance of ongoing enrichment experiences such as marriage conferences and books that challenge you to further growth. But if you and your spouse identify more with where Teresa and I were more than two decades ago, you are acutely aware of the need to reach out for some encouragement, answers, and direction. In either case, working through this book together will be an enriching experience for both of you.

*I*T was the beginning of an intense, sometimes painful, and ultimately fulfilling marital journey for me and Teresa— a journey that continues to this day.

By *marriage enrichment* we're not talking about mastering the hottest new formula for marital bliss or locking on to the top three or four or six proven techniques to marital success. Teresa and I had tried all the surefire, guaranteed-effective keys to enriching marriage—we had even taught them. Despite everything we had learned and tried, something fundamental and vital was missing from our marriage. The love that once sparkled in Teresa's eyes and brightened her face had dimmed, and the closeness I yearned for in our relationship was gone and seemingly out of reach. We were doing all the right things, but we did not know *why* we were doing them. Our lives had become routine, and our love had grown cold. We had lost sight of the purpose of our marriage.

## STRIVING FOR ONENESS

What is the purpose of marriage? You have no doubt heard it said that the purpose of marriage is for a husband and wife to achieve spiritual, emotional, and physical oneness. In Genesis 2:24 God declares, "For this cause a man shall leave his father and his mother, and shall cleave to his wife; and they shall become one flesh." That is what I had been taught—and I fervently taught it to others. I believed that growing into oneness brought greater security, happiness, and fulfillment in marriage. And I still believe that.

But I also believed and taught that oneness was achieved through mastering the latest communication techniques or improving our love language or understanding a spouse's personality traits. And while my teachings on these skills were helpful to many couples, the vitality often faded for them a few weeks after they attended our marriage retreats. After Teresa's shocking revelation of emotional numbness toward me, my confidence in all I had learned, practiced, and taught about marital oneness was shattered. At that point Teresa and I began our search for something more fundamental to achieving oneness than mastering certain techniques and skills.

We found that our marriage was probably deficient in three key areas:

**We needed more of God in our marriage.** We have all heard it said that the family that prays together, stays together. In that vein, we assumed that the closer we got to God, the closer we would get to each other. The more we read our Bibles together, prayed together, attended church together, and grew together spiritually, the deeper our oneness with God would be. And deeper oneness with God should result in deeper oneness with each other. Picture a triangle with the husband and wife at the opposite corners of the base and God at the peak. As spouses move upward toward the peak where God is, they should automatically grow closer together.

Yes, we knew we needed more of God in our marriage. Who

doesn't? But somehow all our Bible reading, praying, and ministry together had not translated into deeper oneness between us. Teresa was emotionally numb, and I was disillusioned. There was still something missing in our relationship.

**We needed more of God's Word in our marriage.** We always believed that the Word of God was our road map to greater oneness in marriage. The Bible laid out our responsibilities as husband and wife and identified our distinct roles as male and female. We assumed that the deeper we got into the Word, the deeper we would get into one another. I had worked hard to commit large portions of Scripture to memory. Teresa and I had diligently studied the Bible together and taught it to others. However, for all our devotion to God's Word, we were not one. Something more was needed.

**We needed to be more other-centered in our marriage.** We believed that we would achieve greater oneness in our marriage if we became less self-centered and more other-centered. Romans 12:2 reads, "Do not be conformed to this world, but be transformed by the renewing of your mind, that you may prove what the will of God is, that which is good and acceptable and perfect." If we continually renewed our minds and began to *think* right toward each other, we should be able to *do* right and grow in oneness.

Changing my focus toward Teresa led me to help around the house more, share her workload, and send flowers to her occasionally, demonstrating that I could be sensitive and considerate. This helped our relationship some, but there was still a vast desert between us. Something was still missing in our understanding of oneness in marriage.

The more we strove for oneness through these important and necessary activities, the more we sensed that we were still at a surface level. We sensed that God had a deeper purpose for marriage, a more fundamental focus for experiencing oneness with each other. As we transparently shared our hopes and desires for our marriage with a few close friends, we found that they shared our longing.

Our striving for oneness had been largely unfruitful, but our longing for oneness drove us on.

## LONGING FOR ONENESS

Having ministered for nearly twenty years to tens of thousands of married couples across America and in Europe, Teresa and I have come to a better understanding of this longing for oneness in marriage. It is a longing placed within each of us by our Creator. We believe there are four intrinsic elements of oneness that every couple desires from their marriage relationship.

**1. We long to deeply know and be known by someone.** God created each of us as relational beings with a need to be known. It is as if God wired into us a yearning for someone to explore the depths of who we really are. We want a soul mate who will probe us deeply to understand our aspirations, dreams, fears, and struggles and yet fully love and accept us no matter what he or she finds. And we long to know and accept another in the same way.

**2. We long to be cherished by someone who ministers to our inner needs.** Most of us can explain what love is. We look to passages like 1 Corinthians 13 and define love in terms of qualities such as patience, kindness, humility, forgiveness, and unselfishness. But how does love respond to the triumphs and tragedies of daily life? What does love say to the spouse who has suffered through a terrible day at work or been hassled by the kids for twelve hours straight? What does love do when a spouse has been rejected by a close friend or demoted at work? How does love respond when a spouse fails or struggles with self-doubt and despair?

The Bible reveals practical ways God has designed for us to lovingly meet these needs in a marriage relationship. For example, when we are brokenhearted, we need *comfort*. When we fail, we need *acceptance*. When we struggle, we need *support*. During times of frustration and rejection, we need *encouragement*. When we are afraid, we need *security*. There are other times when we need *attention, appreciation, affection, respect,* and *approval.* We all long for a cherishing love relationship in which our most basic inner needs can be met.

**3. We long for someone through whom we can experience comfort for life's inevitable hurts.** We live in a pain-filled world in which disappointment, criticism, loss, rejection, and heartache are inevitable. When we experience physical injury or illness, we seek out medical professionals for advice and treatment. But where do we turn for healing when the heart is wounded? Wouldn't it be wonderful if spouses could be loving instruments of God's comfort and healing from our inner wounds—both past and present?

**4. We long to give ourselves freely to someone without fear or reservation.** When life's inevitable disappointments and relational hurts cut deeply or go unhealed, we are often ruled by mistrust and fear of others, even those closest to us. The pain may be from a hurtful childhood episode or from a recent experience. Either way, the baggage of unresolved hurt hinders husbands and wives from giving themselves freely to each other and experiencing deep oneness. Wouldn't it be wonderful to walk free of the baggage and give yourself to your spouse without fear of rejection? Wouldn't it be wonderful to give yourself to him or her without reservation and know that you are fully accepted just as you are? And wouldn't it be wonderful to receive your spouse in the same way?

*DON'T you yearn for the oneness of deeply knowing each other, tenderly cherishing each other, compassionately ministering to each other, and freely giving yourselves to each other?*

Isn't this what you want out of your marriage? Don't you yearn for the oneness of deeply knowing each other, tenderly cherishing each other, compassionately ministering to each other, and freely giving yourselves to each other?

Over our many years of equipping people for Great Command-ment ministry and marriage (loving God above all and loving our neighbors—those people closest and dearest to us—as we love ourselves), Teresa and I have found two major roadblocks between couples and the oneness they seek in marriage. First, most couples cannot clearly define what they want out of their marriage. Second, many couples who *can* nail down what they want soon discover that what they want is unattainable.

We are confident that the four "longings for oneness" are a part of what every couple wants out of marriage. Furthermore, they are realistic and attainable. In the chapters ahead, you will discover that this is what God designed for your marriage. Regardless of where you are in your relationship today, you can experience a wonderfully fulfilling marriage by experiencing the oneness God has waiting for you. Like Teresa and me, you may be surprised at the source for God's oneness in marriage.

## ARE WE ASKING THE WRONG QUESTION?

After Teresa's sobering declaration that she felt nothing for me, we revisited the question, How can we get the most out of our mar-riage?—even though the answer had clearly eluded us for fifteen years. But the more we considered that question, the more God seemed to challenge our motivation. For the first time we were struck with the blatant self-centeredness of the question: What are *we* getting? It occurred to us that God may want to change our mo-tivation for oneness.

The thought so intrigued us that we began an intense Bible study on the topic of God's purpose for marriage. Our study brought us to two arresting truths.

First, we observed in the pages of Scripture that *when God blesses someone, that person experiences abundance.* When God blessed Abraham, he was instrumental in bringing forth a great and mighty nation. When God blessed the children of Israel, they enjoyed bountiful harvests and prospered. When God blessed the armies of Joshua or David, they vanquished their enemies. It is a biblical truth: Whatever and whomever God chooses to bless always enjoy abundant success. Job declared to God, "I know that you can do anything, and no one can stop you" (Job 42:2, NLT). This is the powerful, sovereign God we serve. Teresa and I concluded that if our marriage was going to succeed, we must have God's blessing on it.

Second, we observed that *God promises to bless that which brings him honor and glory.* God is perfectly righteous, and he alone is worthy to receive glory and honor (see Revelation 4:11). He will not bless anything that does not glorify him. This truth prompted a series of startling thoughts about marriage:

God will bless the marriage that brings honor and glory to him.

Therefore God can actually receive honor and glory from a marriage.

When God receives the honor and glory he rightly deserves from the marriage, he blesses it.

And when God blesses the marriage, it experiences abundance, and the oneness for which the couple longs is achieved.

Teresa and I paused to wonder: Were we asking the wrong question? Was our motivation for oneness self-centered when it should be *God-centered?* Instead of asking "How can we get the most out of our marriage?" should we instead be asking, *"What does God want out of our marriage?"*

*G*OD will bless the marriage that brings honor and glory to him.

This question shocked us at first. We had touched on a great mystery. The majestic, all-knowing, all-powerful God, who is complete in himself and needs nothing from us, desires to *receive* from his human creation. He is not egocentric, selfish, or demanding. Yet our compassionate, generous God is capable of receiving from us as we can give glory and honor to him through our marriages.

The implications to Teresa and me were staggering. If we were able to provide honor and glory to God through our marriage, not only would we open ourselves to God's rich blessing, but better still we would fulfill *his purpose for our marriage.* We were gripped by this reality, even sensing God's pleasure in pursuit of what he wants to receive from our marriage.

Over the years we have recognized a similar response in couples whenever we pose this question, "What is God getting out of your marriage?" Heads turn. A few mouths drop open. People respond in wonder, "What was that again?" They are somewhat stunned and awestruck as they consider the question and its possible answers. Perhaps the question affects you the same way.

The fact that God desires something from your marriage suggests that he really cares about the details of your life together. It implies that the God who created marriage for his pleasure wants to be actively involved in every facet of your union. Don't you sense something inspiring and challenging from this truth? You may also sense something of mystery and wonder as you contemplate exactly what it is about your marriage that can honor him.

Teresa and I felt the same way. Intrigued, awed, and inspired at the realization that God could receive something from every relationship, we set out to discover in the pages of Scripture what God desires to receive. This book is the result of that search.

## UNLOCKING THE MYSTERY

The mystery of oneness in marriage seems to begin on the opening page of Scripture with these words: "Let us make people in our image" (Gen. 1:26, NLT). These words suggest that the one true God, who exists in perfect relationship as Father, Son, and Holy Spirit, has chosen to share with us, his human creation, the blessing of oneness in relationship. And this blessing falls first on the relationship between his first created beings—"male and female he created them" (Gen. 1:27, NLT).

In the New Testament, the apostle Paul gives one of the clearest marriage teachings, in which husbands are encouraged to love their wives and wives to respect their husbands (see Ephesians 5:21-33). Oneness between husband and wife is clearly linked to oneness on the higher plane in Paul's conclusion: "As the Scriptures say, 'A man leaves his father and mother and is joined to his wife, and the two are united into one.' This is a great mystery, but it is an illustration of the way Christ and the church are one" (Eph. 5:31-32, NLT). Peter refers to the mysteries of redemption as "things into which angels long to look" (1 Pet. 1:12). In the pages ahead, we will look into the mysteries of marriage, mysteries that even have the angels of heaven curious!

We invite you to join us in the journey to unlock some of the wonderful mysteries of God's love lavished on his human creation. We will explore God's desire to be honored in your marriage and to be actively and intimately involved in your life together. We will discover the biblical guidelines for honoring God in your relationship and realizing the blessing of oneness he promises.

Our hope and prayer as you read this book is that you will grow in awe and wonder that God wants to permeate your marriage and revel in the joy of your unique union. We also pray that you will be motivated to give to him what he seeks from your relationship. As you respond lovingly to him, God's promised blessings await you. We believe you will agree that his blessing on your marriage is beyond anything you have ever imagined. We also believe you will realize a oneness together beyond anything you have ever longed for.

*THE one true God, who exists in perfect relationship as Father, Son, and Holy Spirit, has chosen to share with us, his human creation, the blessing of oneness in relationship.*

# PART
# one

## God's Colleague
### We Are Deeply Known

# CHAPTER 1

# The Mystery of Turning "Not Good" into "Very Good"

Several years after Teresa's shocking disclosure that she felt emotionally numb in our relationship, a small but significant incident affirmed to me that something good was happening in our marriage. The dry desert of distance between us was being gradually replaced by the lush oneness we both craved.

Every year, Teresa and I try to get away to a quiet, comfortable lodge in the Smoky Mountains for a few days. It has become our own personal retreat, where the two of us can relax alone or with a few friends. One year, just before leaving home for the airport and our annual pilgrimage to Tennessee, I passed by the kitchen and sensed God prompting this new thought: *Why don't you take a few packets of Sweet'n Low with you for Teresa?* Over the years of our marriage I have learned that Teresa prefers Sweet'n Low over other sweeteners in her coffee, but the lodge where we usually stay doesn't serve that brand. So I reached into the kitchen cupboard for a handful of pink packets and slipped them into my briefcase.

We arrived at the lodge just in time for dinner. As dessert and coffee were served, Teresa began searching the table for the Sweet'n Low, disappointed again that it wasn't there. But I had come to the table prepared. As I pulled a small pink packet out of my pocket and handed it to her, the disappointment on Teresa's face was washed away by an endearing smile. Tears filled her eyes, and she hugged me. At that moment I relished the pleasure I was able to bring to my wife with such a simple act. I also sensed God's pleasure at what had happened. He seemed to say, "We did well together, David! You needed me to prompt you to bring Sweet'n Low, and I needed you to pick up the packets and share them with Teresa."

I am convinced I never would have thought to bring the Sweet'n Low on my own. Someone else was thinking of Teresa that day, and he wanted to involve me in the ministry of caring for my wife in this special way. God could have prompted the restaurant manager at the lodge to order Sweet'n Low in time to have it available when we arrived. Or God could have miraculously arranged for a pink packet to materialize on the table where we were to be seated. But, amazingly, he invited *me* to be his colleague in this loving act. And when I responded, Teresa and I experienced a new measure of oneness, and the One who loves us both was honored and blessed.

## A COLLEAGUE WITH GOD

This small incident reinforced to Teresa and me how much we needed God in our marriage and how much God desires to be a partner with each of us in the ministry of loving each other. This concept leads us to the first answer to the vital question posed in the introductory chapter: What is God getting out of your marriage? He is seeking a colleague—a dedicated partner and coworker—in the ministry of loving your spouse, and you are the colleague he wants. Furthermore, he is seeking a colleague to join him in the ministry of loving you, and he wants your spouse to fill that role.

And when God receives in you the colleague he seeks, you in turn receive the marvelous benefits of being partnered with him in your marriage. The God who knows your spouse completely is present to share his knowledge of him or her with you. He may not prompt you to slip pink packets into your briefcase, but he will lead you into a deeper understanding of your spouse so you can care for him or her in a similar way. What a wonderful arrangement! God receives a colleague, and you receive a measure of fulfillment for your longing to deeply know and be known by your spouse. This section of the book will fully explore this biblical principle.

But first let's answer another question: Why does God want to partner with us so intimately in marriage? To answer that question we must go back to the beginning. Come with me on an imaginative journey back to a special day in Paradise.

## THE GREAT MYSTERY IN THE GARDEN

It was a perfectly beautiful day. The sun was radiant, and a pleasant breeze ruffled the tall, verdant grass. It was the most beautiful day of Adam's life. Of course, it was only the *first day* of his life.

"What do you think of the Garden?" God asks as he and Adam walk together in the idyllic setting.

"I love it here," Adam answers enthusiastically. "No crime, no traffic, no pollution, no disease, no war. This place is just perfect, isn't it?"

"Yes," God replies, "you live in a perfect world, and you are in charge of it all."

"All?" Adam echoes, and God nods and smiles. "Wow! I am in charge of everything, and I have everything I need. I have fresh air to breathe, a wonderful spring to drink from, plenty of delicious vegetables and fruit to eat—except for that one tree you told me not to eat from. I mean, I've got everything. This is *really* good!"

"Yes, it is good," God affirms. "And what about the responsibilities I gave you?"

"My job? Oh yes, I *love* this job," Adam exults. "You appointed

*G*OD *is seeking a colleague—a dedicated partner and coworker—in the ministry of loving your spouse, and you are the colleague he wants.*

me to be the CEO over the fish, the birds, the livestock, the bugs—all the creatures you created. I guess I'm at the top of the career ladder. Of course, I'm the only one *on* the ladder!"

"But at least you're at the top!" God inserts with a grin.

"Right. I couldn't be happier. No problems with job security, no competition for advancement, and no hassles with coworkers. I guess I have it made. This is so good."

"Adam, what do you like best about the Garden?" God probes as they stroll along.

"That's easy," Adam answers without hesitation. "It's you, Lord. I enjoy the beauty of my surroundings, I enjoy being with the animals, and I enjoy the responsibilities you have given me. But you are my dearest friend. I don't know what I would do without you. Everything here is good, but you are the best."

They walk along in silence for several moments relishing the surroundings and enjoying each other's company. Finally God speaks. "Adam, I am pleased that you like the Garden in which you will live and work. It is all good. But now I need to talk to you about something that is *not* good."

Adam stops abruptly and turns toward the Creator with a cloud of confusion shadowing his face. "I don't understand, Lord. You created the sun, moon, and stars, and they are good. You spoke the land, water, plants, and animals into existence, and they are good. You and I enjoy an intimate and fulfilling relationship. Everything is perfect. What could possibly be not good?"

## WHAT WAS NOT GOOD

*Not good*—the words had never been uttered before. Throughout the Genesis 1 account of the creation, we repeatedly read the words, "God saw that it was good" (see verses 10, 12, 18, 21, 25). Adam lived in a perfect world. He possessed everything he could possibly need or want. God had given him an exalted position. And at this point Adam enjoyed with God an intimate relationship uninterrupted by sin. What could be wrong with this picture? What could be "not good"?

Then God declared, "It is not good for the man to be alone; I will make him a helper suitable for him" (Gen. 2:18). We can imagine Adam responding, "But Lord, I'm *not* alone. I have the Garden and the animals to occupy my time. And most important, I have you."

If God had spoken with Adam on this point, he might have said, "Everything I have made is good, but I am not quite finished with my creative work here. You and I enjoy a very special relationship, and I desire it to continue. But I have also created you for other relationships. Until I provide another being like you, you are alone. And since I did not design you to be alone, it is not good for you to be alone."

What can we derive about the "not good" from Genesis 2:18? Had God made some kind of mistake that had to be corrected? Had he forgotten something? Absolutely not. The Old Testament proclaims, "Ascribe greatness to our God! The Rock! His work is perfect" (Deut. 32:3-4). God makes no mistakes, and he is not forgetful. It is clear that God's masterpiece, as it was described in Genesis 2:18, was not yet complete. He had designed Adam with a capacity for intimate relationship with himself *and* with other human beings. It was all part of God's blueprint for humankind. But until an "other" was there to relate to Adam and complete God's design, it was not good.

Why did God create Adam with a need for other people? Considering what Scripture teaches us about marriage and other relationships, perhaps God explained it something like this: "Adam, I have created all things for my glory, including you. And I have purposely created you with a need for other human relationships, beginning with the helper I will provide for you. As I partner with your helper to remove your aloneness, and partner with you to remove her aloneness, your inner longing for oneness will be fulfilled. I yearn to see you blessed abundantly in this way, and as it happens, a great mystery unfolds: I receive pleasure, and I am blessed."

The Scriptures record the scene of God's final creative act: "So the Lord God caused a deep sleep to fall upon the man, and he slept; then He took one of his ribs, and closed up the flesh at that place. And the Lord God fashioned into a woman the rib which He had taken from the man, and brought her to the man. And the man said, 'This is now bone of my bones, and flesh of my flesh; She shall be called Woman, because she was taken out of Man.' For this cause a man shall leave his father and his mother, and shall cleave to his wife; and they shall become one flesh" (Gen. 2:21-24).

*GOD'S design for oneness is a great and wonderful mystery. It is the mystery of turning the "not good of aloneness" into "very good."*

We can imagine Adam's response to all this. "I am amazed! You, the infinite God, are pleased to enter the finite relationship of a man and woman to fill our need for one another and bring us oneness. This is indeed a great and wonderful mystery."

Yes, God's design for oneness is a great and wonderful mystery. It is the mystery of turning the "not good of aloneness" into "very good." The Bible's summary statement of God's completed work reads, "God saw all that He had made, and behold, it was *very* good" (Gen. 1:31, emphasis added). That which was good was now very good. And that which was not good—Adam's aloneness—had been removed in God's provision of oneness for husband and wife, oneness that brings him honor, glory, and pleasure.

### THE MYSTERY OF "VERY GOOD"

Your loving relationship with your spouse is God's "very good" to remove your aloneness and fill your longing to deeply know and be known by another. As the imaginary conversation in the Garden illustrates, our aloneness is not removed solely through a personal, spiritual relationship with God. And it is not removed solely through the human marriage relationship. The "very good" of God's design for marriage is found in a three-way relationship. God desires that you partner with him in the marriage to remove your spouse's aloneness, and God desires to join with your spouse to remove your aloneness.

Some people protest that God alone meets all our needs, that he doesn't need to involve a spouse to remove our aloneness. They quote Philippians 4:13, "I can do all things through Him who strengthens me." They sing hymns that celebrate God's total sufficiency, hymns like "Jesus Is All I Need." They firmly insist, "I have God, and God meets all my needs."

Teresa and I wholeheartedly believe that God is the ultimate source for meeting all our needs. We understand both biblically and experientially our deep need for God. Nothing else—not possessions, not position, not success, not another person—can fill the God-shaped vacuum within each of us. God alone brings peace and order to the human heart. Yet God revealed a wondrous mystery in the Garden. In his unsearchable wisdom, he has chosen to partner with us to remove the "not good" of aloneness in our spouses. He is still the source for taking away the "not good" of being alone in our marriages, but he desires to enlist us as his colleagues in the process.

*G*OD *desires that you partner with him in the marriage to remove your spouse's aloneness, and God desires to join with your spouse to remove your aloneness.*

What about people who are not married? Is God's design for removing aloneness thwarted in those who are single? Absolutely not. God's wonderful plan for removing human aloneness is fulfilled in three divinely appointed relationships. For those who are married, the marriage relationship is God's primary means for removing aloneness. But some people do not marry, and some marriages do not continue. In such cases, loving family—parents, children, grandparents, siblings—is a divinely provided relationship for removing aloneness. In time, Adam and Eve produced Cain, Abel, Seth, and other children. They in turn had their own families to remove their aloneness. The psalmist explains, "Children are a gift from the Lord; they are a reward from him" (Ps. 127:3, NLT). The family is to be a loving, cherishing environment where the aloneness of each member is removed by the others.

And for those who for some reason are without close family, God's "safety net" for removing human aloneness is his body, the church. Jesus declared, "By this all men will know that you are My disciples, if you have love for one another" (John 13:35). God has graciously provided marriage, family, and the body of Christ so that no one should suffer the "not good" of being alone.


I NEEDED ONLY GOD

At age twenty-one, I was fully aware of my personal need for God, and that is when I trusted him as my Savior and when his Spirit began rapid changes in my heart and life. As I began to grow as a Christian, I generally accepted the idea that I needed other people somehow. But I firmly believed that my only *real* need was for God. And I assumed that if others—including Teresa—would just become more spiritual, they would not need me! This view skewed my understanding of God's design for involving me in removing Teresa's aloneness. And I certainly didn't understand God's desire to remove my aloneness through Teresa. Since God had not found in me a colleague to care for Teresa, the oneness she and I sought was elusive, and the blessing God desired and deserved from our relationship was limited.

As growing Christians eager to do God's work, Teresa and I

poured ourselves into spiritual pursuits. I memorized large portions of Scripture. I became deeply involved in a ministry to students, and I led discipleship groups. Teresa became involved in her own ministry, which reached thousands of women each year. Eventually Teresa and I conducted marriage seminars together. In our efforts to please God and serve others, our primary focus and priority was on ministry. By placing my ministry before our marriage, I left Teresa alone. By placing our children and her ministry before our marriage, Teresa left me alone. Although our church viewed us as the ideal ministry couple, we continued to silently endure our relationship. We were very active and very busy, but very alone.

In those years I was so focused on my spiritual life and ministry that I had little time or attention for my family. Teresa was left with the responsibility of caring for our two daughters, Terri and Robin, and our young son, Eric. Occasionally she would lament to me her desire for a more loving husband and a more devoted father for our children. But my attitude said, "Teresa, you don't need more of me to have a fulfilling life; you need more of God."

## WE ALL NEED GOD AND ONE ANOTHER

It is true that a relationship with God is to be primary in each of our lives. We are to trust Christ as Savior, yield to his Spirit, and obey his words: " 'You must love the Lord your God with all your heart, all your soul, and all your mind.' This is the first and greatest commandment" (Matt. 22:37-38, NLT). Had Jesus stopped there, we might conclude that all we need is a relationship with God. But Jesus went on: "A second is equally important: 'Love your neighbor as yourself.' All the other commandments and all the demands of the prophets are based on these two commandments" (Matt. 22:39-40, NLT). In Jesus' eyes, relationship with our neighbors—literally our "near ones"—is as important as relationship with God.

As we set our hearts on loving God completely, he desires to enlist us as his colleagues to remove the aloneness of our near ones, beginning with our spouses. Teresa and I often call this the Great Commandment marriage—loving God with all your heart and loving your spouse—your nearest near one—as yourself (see also Ephesians 5:28). Removing aloneness is a fundamental purpose of marriage. Are you God's colleague actively involved in the process of removing your spouse's aloneness? Is your spouse less alone today than he or she has ever been? This is an important biblical measure of a successful marriage relationship.

It is clear throughout Scripture that God, for reasons known only to him, has opted to fill our longings for oneness through love relationships with both himself *and* other human beings. He is totally sufficient in his provision, but in his sovereignty he has chosen to share some of his love through the three relationships he has ordained: marriage, family, and the church. If we are not fulfilling the Great Commandment in our marriages, our families, or in our churches, the result is not good.

## WHY IT IS NOT GOOD TO BE ALONE

As Teresa and I travel and teach about Great Commandment marriage, we talk to countless Christian couples who are married but still alone. Most of them struggle, as we did, in clinging to the notion that our deep longings for oneness in marriage can be fulfilled only in a direct, personal relationship with God. We failed to understand God's desire to become our colleague to remove aloneness in our relationship with each other. As we continued in this misperception, we experienced the emptiness and pain of missing God's best in our relationship, and our life together was not good.

During one of our conferences for ministry leaders, a pastor approached Teresa and me to share his wife's problem. "She is a bundle of fear, anxiety, and insecurity," he explained. "She's afraid of flying, afraid of the dark, afraid of driving in traffic, afraid of strangers, afraid of . . . practically everything. Being so fearful and paranoid, she tries to control everything and everyone around her. She figures that if she can be in complete control of her life, she won't be afraid. She controls not only her own schedule and activities but also my life and our kids' lives. If the beds are not made perfectly or the dishes are not loaded into the dishwasher just so, she blows up at us. She's driving us crazy."

Before he could say something like "Do you think you could fix her?" I said, "Pastor, we know what removes fear, don't we?"

He was silent and looked puzzled, so I rephrased my question in terms more familiar to him. "We know what *casts out* fear, don't we?"

He flashed a look of comprehension. Shifting into his preacher's voice, he responded, "That's what I have been trying to tell her. Perfect love casts out fear."

"And whose love is perfect, Pastor?" I continued.

"God's love," he answered, as if preaching it from the pulpit.

"Pastor, where has God put some of his perfect love that will cast out your wife's fear?"

Catching the drift of my question, he started backing away. "Hey, I didn't think I would have to be involved in this!"

How did this man come to such a conclusion? He was locked in the common belief that his wife needed only God to solve her problem. But underneath this wife's fear, insecurity, and control issues was a woman who was very alone. This pastor was blind to the fact that God wanted to enlist him as a colleague in loving his wife, casting out her fear, and removing her aloneness. As a result, their marriage and family life were in shambles. She was alone, and it was not good.

The "not good" of aloneness may take many forms in a marriage relationship. When we do not experience God's blessing

*IN Jesus' eyes, relationship with our neighbors—literally our "near ones"—is as important as relationship with God.*

and provision for our aloneness, we become *vulnerable to discouragement.* Many couples struggle under the pressure of strained finances, territorial fights, and threats of leaving. Many more suffer in silence. Many couples do not plan goals together or try to solve problems together. Struggling through tough times alone, they sometimes feel they are no better off than couples who divorce and start over with someone new. Solomon's wisdom answers: "Two people can accomplish more than twice as much as one; they get a better return for their labor. If one person falls, the other can reach out and help. But people who are alone when they fall are in real trouble" (Eccles. 4:9-10, NLT).

When we do not experience God's blessing and provision for removing aloneness, we become *vulnerable to temptation.* Some husbands who are alone in their marriages are drawn into pornography, which can lead to sexual addiction. Some wives who are alone seek intimacy through sleazy romance novels and soap operas, which set the stage for illicit affairs. In this high-tech age, an increasing number of men and women are leaving their spouses for people they meet and "fall in love with" in Internet chat rooms. Again Solomon responds. "If two lie down together they keep warm, but how can one be warm alone?" (Eccles. 4:11).

When we do not experience God's blessing and provision for our aloneness, we become *vulnerable to defeat.* Many homes are being torn apart by anger, reprisal, rejection, and out-of-control children as defeat replaces God's plan for victory in relationships. The enemy runs roughshod over the marriage and family divided by aloneness. Solomon reminds us, "A person standing alone can be attacked and defeated, but two can stand back-to-back and conquer. Three are even better, for a triple-braided cord [God, you, and your spouse] is not easily broken" (Eccles. 4:12, NLT).

Teresa and I believe that most, if not all, of the personal, family, and social crises plaguing our culture today can be traced to the "not good" of relational aloneness. A few years ago I attended a conference convened to discuss the local impact of the numerous crises of our culture. The conference—which was secular, not Christian—was attended by civic leaders and local politicians. Also represented were a number of secular organizations and agencies formed to deal with such issues as crime, teenage pregnancy, substance abuse, school dropouts, and domestic abuse.

As the participants began to discuss the symptoms and the root causes, a consensus arose—which is something of a miracle in a group of headstrong leaders. They concurred that underneath the many and varied social problems plaguing our community was one common dilemma: the breakdown of the family. As significant as their conclusion was, the conference participants did not stop there. They advanced a thesis to identify the cause of the ills of society and the disintegration of the family. Here's what they decided: People are more alienated and isolated from each other than ever before. The outward manifestations of crime, drugs, rebellion, abuse, addiction, and family breakup spring from feelings of emptiness, lack of love, insecurity, discouragement, frustration, and aloneness.

Teresa and I could not agree more. And statistics confirm the diagnosis: Alienation and disconnectedness between individuals is widespread. Significant portions of the adult population today grew up suffering from some form of parental separation, abandonment, or addiction, and possibly from physical or sexual abuse that has left them alienated and disconnected. And when that aloneness, no matter what the cause, is not removed, it is not good.

In response to this diagnosis, some people may protest, "What about sin? Isn't sin at the heart of society's ills?" Yes, sin is real, pervasive, and devastating. Adam and Eve

*MOST, if not all, of the personal, family, and social crises plaguing our culture today can be traced to the "not good" of relational aloneness.*

and everyone since have disobeyed God. Sin is what keeps us alone, separated from God and others. God's burden and provision for sin are related to this truth. He knows that sin keeps us alone and that aloneness brings forth the "not good" of relational strife and pain. No wonder his heart is full of compassion for us. No wonder he acted to remedy the consequences of sin that keep us alone.

## HOW GOD KNOWS ALONENESS IS NOT GOOD

How does God know that being alone is not good? Being an omniscient God, does he then intrinsically know that aloneness is not good? Or did God make his pronouncement from an *experiential* knowledge, having personally tasted the "not good" of being alone?

Some people struggle with the concept that God could personally experience being alone. They contend that the triune God has never been alone in all of eternity. They refer to the Godhead who said at creation, "Let Us make man in Our image, according to Our likeness" (Gen. 1:26). They point out that God is the perfect unity of Father, Son, and Holy Spirit.

That's true. But we are talking about the God who is not confined to time and history as we experience it. When he declared in the Garden, "It is not good for the man to be alone" (Gen. 2:18), had he not already experienced the crisis of Calvary? In his eternal existence, had the Father not already heard his Son cry out in agony, "My God, my God, why have you forsaken me?" (Matt. 27:46, NLT)? Had the Father not already experienced the heartpiercing pain of being separated from his only Son?

I believe he had. And this is how God could say to Adam with authority that aloneness is not good. God knew experientially what it means to be alone. From eternity past, the Father knew the pain and emptiness of being separated from his Son. This is part of why he so compassionately calls you to become his colleague in removing your spouse's aloneness.

Recently a young married couple came to Teresa and me and announced that they were struggling with the idea of a God who could understand their relational aloneness. The wife, Emily, said to me, "David, I'm sorry, but I just can't imagine that God feels any pain for me or my marriage. I don't think it's biblical."

As I reached for my Bible, I asked Emily if she thought God could feel sad over the hurt that sin has caused his creation. She hesitated and then said, "I'm sure he doesn't like it."

"Yes," I agreed, "I'm sure he doesn't like what sin has caused. But do you think he is saddened by it?"

"I'm not sure," she replied.

I said, "Let me read to you how God felt about his creation at the time of Noah." I read Genesis 6:5-6: "The Lord saw how great man's wickedness on the earth had become, and that every inclination of the thoughts of his heart was only evil all the time. The Lord was grieved that he had made man on the earth, and his heart was filled with pain" (NIV).

I looked at Emily and asked, "These verses tell us that God was grieved and his heart was filled with pain. Can you not imagine a compassionate God hurting because of what sin and aloneness had done to the creation he loved?"

She shook her head slowly and replied, "It's hard for me to see God hurting."

After a pause, I probed, "Why, Emily? Why is it hard for you to see a God who hurts for you?"

"Because when I hurt, I lose control, and I can't imagine God losing control."

Emily was laboring under a distorted picture of God. When God experiences the pain of aloneness and sin, he does not lose control. There is nothing irrational or impulsive about him or his behavior. When he experienced personally the pain of sin and aloneness caused by his human creation, he did not lose control or act irrationally. Rather, his fathomless love compelled him to send his only Son to die an awful death for us. God is an omnipotent God, but he is also a relationally relevant God. "For we do not have a high priest who cannot sympathize with our weaknesses, but One who has been tempted in all things as we are, yet without sin" (Heb. 4:15).

God longs to enter your marriage and involve you and your spouse as his colleagues in removing the aching void of aloneness because he knows experientially that it is not good to be alone. As the triune God, he also knows the "very good" of oneness in a loving relationship. And when the "not good" of aloneness is replaced by the "very good" of oneness that he introduced in the Garden, he is pleased.

*G*OD longs to enter your marriage and involve you and your spouse as his colleagues in removing the aching void of aloneness because he knows experientially that it is not good to be alone.

As God and Adam walked in the Garden together, God declared aloneness to be "not good." When Eve was added to the population as Adam's helper, God declared his finished work to be very good. At first glance, we might assume that "not good" became "very good" simply at the addition of another human being. But that is no more true than to assume that any man and woman who say "I do" will automatically enjoy a very good marriage.

The "not good" of aloneness in a marriage relationship is removed only as each spouse becomes God's colleague in the process of deeply knowing and being known by the other. In the following pages, you will discover how becoming God's colleague brings him pleasure and transforms "not good" into "very good" in your marriage.

# CHAPTER 2

# Intimate Relationships Remove Aloneness

Teresa and I were both sixteen years old and still in high school when we got married, and neither of us was a Christian at the time. The whirlwind romance began with our first date. We went out for a Coke, and then I took Teresa with me to the county jail to visit a crazy buddy of mine. This guy's goal in life was to see the inside of every jail in the state of Texas as an inmate! Perhaps I wanted to impress my new girlfriend by showing her that I hung out with people who had clear goals in life.

Despite a less-than-romantic beginning, Teresa and I fell in love. Six months later, we faced our parents with a rebellious ultimatum: "We have decided to get married. If you don't give your permission, we will elope to Kansas, where marriage at our age is legal." Our parents shed tears at our wedding, but they were not tears of joy.

Teresa and I spent our wedding night in a local motel. Early the next morning while Teresa was still asleep, a friend of mine knocked on the door of our room. Stanley and I were pool-shooting buddies, and he wanted me to go shoot pool with him. The fact that I was on my honeymoon didn't seem to matter to Stanley, and it didn't make much difference to me. I loved shooting pool, so I got dressed, and we left for the pool hall. It never entered my mind to tell Teresa, who was still asleep when I walked out the door.

Teresa tells what happened next: "When I woke up and found David and his car gone, I didn't know what to think. Had I displeased him already? Had he changed his mind about being married to me? I was only sixteen years old, and I felt confused and abandoned. So I left the motel and walked the several blocks home to my parents, crying and feeling very alone."

Somehow Teresa and I survived that rocky beginning. But I had communicated through my behavior that she was not the only thing in my life—and sometimes not even the most important thing. Without the tools to deal with such deep insensitivity and selfishness on my part, Teresa buried her pain, and we simply carried on with life. That honeymoon experience was in effect the first truckload of sand in what would grow to become the Ferguson Desert over the next fifteen years.

Obviously, God desired much more for us from our marriage than what we experienced during those fifteen years. He wanted our relationship to remove the aloneness we both felt. He wanted us to experience the oneness for which he created us and for which we both longed. Even though I could not verbalize what was happening inside me at the time, the more Teresa moved away from me, the more alone and needy I felt. Having trusted Christ after five years of marriage and launched into ministry activities, I had hoped that my diligence in spiritual things would somehow resolve my family issues. But it did not.

God had something else in mind, and he graciously began to let us in on his plan. I gradually began to see my ministry and family relationships from his perspective. Long before the Sweet'n Low incident in the Smoky Mountains, God opened my eyes to his concern for the aloneness both Teresa and I had endured for fifteen years. I was about to receive an invitation to become his colleague in knowing and loving Teresa.

ONENESS WITH GOD LEADS TO ONENESS IN MARRIAGE
In the ten years of my Christian life to that point, I had considered
myself to be a devoted student of the Word. I read and studied the
Bible daily. As I transitioned into pastoral ministry, exegeting
Scripture passages and defending the Word were high priorities to
me. I also considered myself something of an expert on family relationships. I preached on the scriptural roles of husbands and wives.
I even conducted seminars on marriage and family enrichment. I
*understood* what Scripture taught about my relationship with
Teresa, but I did *not* understand that I needed Christ as my colleague in expressing his love to my wife.

Then God called me to a journey of *experiencing in my marriage*
the Bible texts that I had preached and taught to others. All
through my ministry life I believed that I must be diligent in the
Lord's work whether or not my family suffered. This was the sacrifice I thought I must make for the cause of the gospel. But God began to show me through his Word that I could not expect success
in my ministry to others if I was not participating with him in my
marriage to experience oneness with Teresa.

The first of a number of passages God
used to confront me was 1 Peter 3:7: "Husbands, in the same way be considerate as you
live with your wives, and treat them with respect as the weaker partner and as heirs with
you of the gracious gift of life, so that nothing will hinder your prayers" (NIV). As this
verse penetrated my heart, I realized that my
relationship with Teresa had a direct impact
on my relationship with God. Failure to be
considerate of her and respect her would result in my prayers being hindered. And how
far will any ministry go without answered
prayers?

*GOD began to
show me
through his Word
that I could not
expect success in my
ministry to others
if I was not
participating with
him in my marriage
to experience
oneness with Teresa.*

33

I remember voicing my response to God in the form of a question: "Are you saying that I should pursue oneness in my relationship with Teresa just as I seek oneness with you? Are you saying that oneness with you is integrally related to oneness with my wife?"

He forcefully impressed his answer on me one evening as Teresa and I were hosting a Bible study in our home. On this particular evening we were discussing how our concept of God is often shaped by our childhood experiences. I asked the people in the circle to share an early memory about their fathers. We went all the way around the circle, each person sharing memories. Finally it was Teresa's turn. She told a story I had never heard before. Here it is, in her words.

"With six children in our home, sometimes my parents didn't seem to have enough attention to meet all our needs. To complicate matters, three of my siblings were hearing impaired, requiring special attention. So as a five-year-old, I remember craving my daddy's attention and being disappointed when he had so little left for me. Every evening just before Daddy arrived home from work, I got very anxious. I remember thinking, *Maybe Daddy will play with me when he gets home tonight.* But he rarely did, and I often went to bed in tears.

"One Saturday morning I woke up early, realizing that Daddy didn't have to go to work that day. My brothers and sisters were not awake yet, so I wandered through the quiet house looking for my daddy. He was not inside, so I went outside, first to the front yard, then around to the back. I spied him on top of the house getting ready to put on a new roof. As usual, he didn't notice me watching him. I remember going to the ladder and climbing it rung by rung to the roof—a very scary activity for a five-year-old. But I looked past the fear because this was my chance for Daddy's attention. I just wanted to be with him."

As Teresa shared her touching story, something profound began to happen in me. I began to experience a measure of God's sorrow and compassion for Teresa. A deep sadness rose in my heart as I pictured that neglected little girl climbing to the top of the house because she missed her daddy. But I felt more than sadness over Teresa's lack of childhood attention. God was allowing me to see Teresa's pain through his eyes. His Spirit was enabling me to feel compassion for her with his heart. He was allowing me to experience the sorrow *he* felt for that neglected little girl.

After that night's Bible study meeting I said to Teresa, "I feel so sad that you missed out on your daddy's attention. You must have felt so alone." As we sat together, she told me more about how alone she felt as a child. As she talked, God's sorrow flooded my heart over how my wrong priorities over the years had so often hurt Teresa in many of these same ways. Just as Teresa's father had withheld much of the attention she needed, I had also robbed her of attention by putting my life and ministry ahead of her. I sensed her pain from the emotional wounds I had unwittingly inflicted over our fifteen years together.

My eyes were opened to see Teresa in a brand-new way—from the perspective of God's compassionate heart for her. He drew near to share with me what he already knew about Teresa and her deep pain. He made me aware of her deep need for a loving, attentive husband and for comfort from both me and a compassionate God. I felt the heart-wrenching ache of her aloneness, and it broke my heart. I pulled Teresa to me and wept for her, just as I felt God was weeping for her. I confessed my part in adding to her pain.

In those moments of closeness I became a colleague with the God of all comfort, who was ministering healing to Teresa's pain. She experienced the blessing of being cared for by God through her husband at that mo-

*MY eyes were opened to see Teresa in a brand-new way—from the perspective of God's compassionate heart for her.*

ment. I was blessed as God shared his loving comfort through me. And as I held Teresa, comforted her, and wept, I sensed that God was also blessed!

Right then, I realized a new call from God. I heard him speak these familiar words to my heart: "Take My yoke upon you, and learn from Me, for I am gentle and humble in heart; and you [and Teresa] shall find rest for your souls" (Matt. 11:29). I sensed that Christ was inviting me to join him in the yoke as his colleague in the ministry of removing Teresa's aloneness.

## JOIN HIM IN THE YOKE AND LEARN

The image of the yoke was common in Jesus' day. A working pair of oxen would be harnessed together side by side under a wooden bar, called a yoke, laid across their necks. A younger ox was often yoked with a more mature ox, who steadied the team and "taught" his less experienced "colleague" how to work in tandem. In using this image, Jesus invites his followers into a productive relationship, joining with him to learn from him and minister with him.

Christ's invitation to join him in the yoke includes joining him in blessing your spouse. He wants you to be his colleague in the ministry of deeply knowing your spouse and removing his or her aloneness. Christ has been loving your spouse all along, but perhaps he has been loving him or her alone because you have not joined him in the yoke. He wants you to learn from him what he knows about your spouse and how to love him or her. He wants you to be teamed with him in his compassionate ministry of removing your spouse's aloneness.

When you accept his invitation, he receives you as the colleague he desires. As his partner in the yoke, you benefit from his thorough knowledge of your spouse. He will reveal to you areas in which your spouse is alone, just as he helped me see the pain of Teresa's childhood. As you cooperate with God in this close relationship, your spouse is blessed, and God receives the honor and glory he deserves.

One of the first things we learn from Christ, our colleague in marriage, is that he does not accomplish his work through a list of principles or keys to marital success, no matter how biblically sound they may be. Information, facts, logic, and rational thought do not remove aloneness, because *aloneness is an issue of the human heart, not an issue of the rational mind.* You cannot program oneness; it must be experienced emotionally and relationally.

Let me illustrate the contrast in the following way. Imagine that you have just walked into a large reception hall jammed with more than three hundred people you have never met. Everybody is talking to everybody else, but nobody is paying attention to you because you are a stranger in this crowd. You probably feel a little left out and alone, right?

Someone might say to you, "There are over three hundred nice people in the room. They are conversing all around you. You can't take a step in any direction without bumping into someone. How can you feel alone?" Would the argument make you feel any better? Probably not. The fact that you are surrounded by people doesn't make you feel any less alone. The only way for your aloneness to be removed in this situation is for someone to show interest in you personally or engage you in conversation. It

*INFORMATION, facts, logic, and rational thought do not remove aloneness, because aloneness is an issue of the human heart, not an issue of the rational mind.*

doesn't matter how many people are there; unless someone demonstrates convincingly that he or she is there *for you,* you will likely feel alone in the crowd.

Similarly, you can memorize every verse about marriage in the Bible and read every Christian marriage book in the store. You may understand every nuance of male and female roles and master every technique that guarantees a successful marriage. But unless your efforts toward oneness move from the intellect to the heart, you and your spouse will still be very alone.

Take Albert and Evelyn, for example. Albert was a fine Christian man who loved his wife and three children. He had a good job, provided well for his family, and stayed home most evenings with Evelyn and the kids.

Yet Evelyn admitted that her relationship with Albert had leveled off and that their marriage seemed lifeless. They were doing just about everything right as a couple. They talked together about their kids' educational, emotional, and spiritual development. They generally agreed about household finances. They were involved together in their church. But in all the busyness of work, raising a family, and church activities, Evelyn felt that she and Albert had somehow drifted apart.

"He's here, but he's not here, if you know what I mean," she lamented to Teresa and me. "I love Albert, and I believe he loves me. But I feel a distance that I can't put my finger on. There seems to be a part of him I can't reach, a part I really want to connect with. And I think he wants that connection too."

What we are really talking about here is *intimacy*. For all that was good in their marriage, Albert and Evelyn were missing out on the oneness—or intimacy—God intended for them to experience in their relationship. An intimate relationship is characterized by a sense of closeness, connectedness, openness, transparency, and vulnerability. One reason Christ invites us into an intimate relationship with him as a colleague is to learn from him how to deepen the intimacy of our relationship with our spouse.

INTIMACY FROM GOD'S PERSPECTIVE

Three Old Testament Hebrew words help us understand intimacy in relationships. These words will help you better understand what

Christ wants you to learn from him as you become his colleague in your marriage.

**The intimacy of deeply knowing your spouse.** The first word is *yada,* meaning "to know." It speaks of deep and intimate acquaintance. In Jeremiah 1:5, God says to the prophet, "Before I formed you in the womb I *knew* you" (emphasis added). God was intimately acquainted with you before you were born, and he wants to teach you how to deeply know your spouse, how to become more intimately acquainted with him or her.

This element of intimacy was largely missing from Evelyn and Albert's relationship. Evelyn later confided to us that she longed for Albert to get to know her for who she really was, not just her roles as wife and mother. She wanted to share with him her aspirations and dreams, her fears and struggles. But Albert showed little interest in such intimacy, and Evelyn's aloneness deepened, making her increasingly vulnerable to temptation. After seventeen years of marriage, Evelyn found a male coworker who seemed more than interested in listening to her pour out her hopes and dreams. Their emotional intimacy opened the door to physical intimacy and an illicit affair. Today Evelyn and Albert are divorced, and Evelyn is more alone than ever.

God created each one of us with a need to be deeply known by others. Something within us cries out, "Please know me!" This cry is like the warning light on the dashboard of your car. If you don't respond to it soon, something "not good" will happen to your car. When our inner cry for intimacy is not addressed, something "not good" is the result. In a marriage relationship you have two people who long to be known and who have the opportunity to become Christ's colleagues in filling that longing. And when one or both spouses fail to pursue an increasingly intimate acquaintance with the

*G*OD *created each one of us with a need to be deeply known by others.*

other, they each in their own way suffer the "not good" of being alone.

Dan, a friend of ours, told us that his fifteen-year marriage seemed to be going nowhere. He said, "The spark has gone out of our relationship. Our life is a dull routine. It's as if I already know everything there is to know about Sarah."

Dan was wrong. Becoming intimately acquainted with your spouse is a never-ending process. The psalmist David said, "You [God] made all the delicate, inner parts of my body and knit me together in my mother's womb. Thank you for making me so wonderfully complex!" (Ps. 139:13-14, NLT). God made each of us "wonderfully complex," so there is more for Dan to know about Sarah than he could discover in one hundred and fifty years, let alone fifteen! Thankfully, Dan awakened to the mysteries of deeply knowing his wife. He later said, "I was so blind to who Sarah really is. It would take me more than a lifetime to discover everything about her."

Christ invites you into the yoke with him to learn some of the mysteries of deeply knowing and being known by your spouse. He wants to share with you what he knows about your spouse and remind you about what you already know. He wants you close enough that he can impress on your heart ways to become his colleague in loving your spouse. The Sweet'n Low incident was one way God ministered through me to remove some of Teresa's aloneness. For you, he may prompt something else. For example:

When you pour yourself a cup of coffee, pour her a cup too.

He's having a tough day. His favorite supper dish would be a nice surprise.

Leave a caring message on her voice mail.

He likes it sometimes when you initiate the lovemaking.

Buy that little trinket she pointed out to you at the mall.

Put the remote control on his side of the sofa.

**The intimacy of transparently disclosing yourself to your**

**spouse.** Proverbs 3:32 says of the Lord, "He is intimate with the upright." *Intimate* in this verse is the Hebrew word *sod,* meaning vulnerable or transparent disclosure. The verse literally means that God discloses himself to us. We are in relationship with a God who not only knows *us* completely but also wants us to know *him* to the point that he discloses himself to us.

We see God's transparent self-disclosure in the Incarnation: "The Word became flesh, and dwelt among us, and we beheld His glory" (John 1:14). Jesus explained to his disciples, "No longer do I call you slaves, for the slave does not know what his master is doing; but I have called you friends, for all things that I have heard from My Father I have made known to you" (John 15:15). We could not have known God if he had not opened himself to us and allowed us to know him.

*WE are in relationship with a God who not only knows us completely but also wants us to know him to the point that he discloses himself to us.*

Intimacy in a marriage relationship involves getting to know your spouse *(yada) and* allowing your spouse to know you *(sod).* Vulnerable self-disclosure means that you share with your spouse your hopes, dreams, joys, and fears. It means that you communicate openly your needs and desires in the relationship. The double-sided intimacy of deeply knowing and being known by your spouse is vital to removing aloneness in your marriage.

**The intimacy of being caringly involved in each other's lives.** The psalmist David declares, "O Lord, Thou . . . art intimately acquainted with all my ways" (Ps. 139:1-3). The Hebrew word *sakan,* translated "intimately" here, connotes caring involvement. David rejoices that the God who had searched him and who knew him (see Psalm 139:1) was also caringly involved in his life. We can make the same claim. God our Creator, who knows us thoroughly and who has allowed us to know him through the Incarnation of his Son, is also intimately and caringly involved in our lives.

God went to extraordinary lengths to assure you that he knows you completely. In his omniscience, of course, he knew every detail about you before you were born. But that's only the beginning. God left heaven to enter the womb of a teenage girl from a working-class family and was born with flesh and bone, just like you. The all-sufficient One became as dependent on his human parents as you were on your parents. The One who created the first human being had to learn to walk as a toddler, just as you did. The One who spoke the worlds into being had to learn to speak as a young child, just as you did. Almighty God cares for you so much that he became like you to demonstrate that he knows *experientially* what it's like to be you! Having experienced everything you experience except for your sin (see Hebrews 4:15), he demonstrates that he knows how to be caringly involved in your joy and pain.

God experienced human discouragement so you would know he is able to lovingly encourage you. He experienced rejection so you would know he is able to lovingly accept you. He experienced physical and emotional pain so you would know he is able to lovingly comfort you. And most significantly, though he did not sin, he *became* sin in order that you could "become the righteousness of God in him" (2 Cor. 5:21).

As a married couple, you are also the recipient of God's caring involvement. He knows about your tough times together and caringly endures with you—for better or for worse. He knows about your financial challenges and caringly overcomes with you—for richer or for poorer. He knows about your physical limitations and caringly perseveres with you—in sickness and in health.

Since God knows you and your spouse thoroughly, he is the perfect colleague for your marriage. He can share with you what he knows about your spouse so you can be caringly involved with him or her. I believe that's what was happening in the

Sweet'n Low episode I described in chapter 1. I already knew that Teresa preferred Sweet'n Low and that our lodge didn't serve that brand. But God, knowing how blessed Teresa would be to have someone take thought of her, prompted me to take some packets to the mountains for her. He was calling me to be caringly involved with him to nurture intimacy with my wife. And as I activated what I knew through caring involvement, Teresa *was* blessed and a measure of her aloneness was removed.

*A*LMIGHTY *God cares for you so much that he became like you to demonstrate that he knows experientially what it's like to be you!*

Caring involvement is the desired response to deeply knowing your spouse and vulnerably disclosing yourself to him or her. You need to intimately *know* your spouse in order to intimately *care for* your spouse. Your spouse needs to intimately *know* you so he or she can intimately *care for* you. And Christ is at the heart of it all. He knows and cares for your spouse, but he does not want to do so alone, so he invites you to join him. He knows and loves you, but he does not want to do so alone, so he invites your spouse to join him. As you slip into the yoke with him and become his colleague in his caring ministry to your spouse, aloneness is removed and intimacy is experienced.

## AN INVITATION TO THE YOKE

As God the Father looks down on your marriage, what does he see? Does he find his Son loving your spouse alone, or does he find you and Christ ministering together as colleagues to remove your spouse's aloneness?

Imagine Jesus standing before you right now, gazing intently at you. His eyes are full of compassion. His arms are lifted in your direction, and resting in his strong hands is a well-worn wooden yoke. He glances down at the yoke and then returns his gaze to you. His look says it all. He longs to do something—something that involves two people, just as the yoke is carved for the necks of two oxen. But Jesus stands alone, beckoning you with eyes warm and intense with compassion.

You know beyond all doubt that the Savior is thoroughly involved in loving your spouse. He is taking thought of him or her daily, moment by moment. He thrills with every joy and success your spouse experiences. And he sorrows over every hurt, every slight, every rejection, every need your spouse suffers. He longs to engage you in his caring ministry to your spouse. But the empty yoke in his hands rocks you with the reality that Christ is loving your spouse all alone!

Then he speaks. Can you hear his invitation?

"Do you want to get to know your spouse at a deeper level, really know this one who shares your life? Your partner is wonderfully complex, but I will help you learn about this person. You need me for this, and I desire you as my colleague. I love your life partner, and I want to express my love through you by helping you know your dear one deeply. As you join your heart with my compassionate heart, I will prompt you in those areas that will provide caring involvement in your partner's life.

"You also need me to empower you for allowing your spouse to know you. Vulnerable self-disclosure is not easy, but I long to love you through your partner as you share with this one who you really are. As you open up your heart and share yourself with your dear one, I am even more free to provide caring involvement through your partner.

"Come and join me in the journey of a deeper, more intimate relationship with your spouse. Take the yoke with me and be my colleague in the ministry of knowing and being known by your dear

44

one. Your growing oneness will bring me great joy, and it will bring you great blessing."

Can you hear his personal invitation to you to join him in the ministry of loving your spouse? Do you sense your need to learn from him? Are you touched by his desire to be an intimate part of your marriage? Are you in awe that your marriage can bring him so much joy?

Why not pause right now and respond to his invitation. Share with him how you feel about the awesome privilege of becoming his colleague in your marriage. Tell him about your love for your spouse, and tell him how you want to learn from him how to deepen that love.

For Teresa and me, a meditation like this brings fresh realization of how much God cares for us as individuals and as a couple. It reinforces to us how deeply he is committed to involving us in the ministry of his compassionate heart. Isn't your heart filled with gratitude to a God who cares so deeply about you and your spouse?

Think about this: You and your spouse have been uniquely called to deeply know one another and remove each other's aloneness. Of the six billion people who populate this planet, no one else has been called to caring involvement with your spouse as you have, and no one else has been called to caring involvement with you as your spouse has. And the God who created you and ordained marriage to remove your aloneness is in your midst. He invites you to join with him in fulfilling the unique call you cannot fulfill alone. Are you not humbled and blessed at the prospect of being Christ's colleague in caring for your spouse in your marriage?

*YOU and your spouse have been uniquely called to deeply know one another and remove each other's aloneness.*

# CHAPTER 3

# Barriers to Intimacy

I t happened on a Monday during the "desert years" of our marriage. Teresa's car was not running, so we had only one car to
get me to work and for Teresa to transport the three children
to school and day care. We all had to leave together that morning,
so I quickly got myself ready and went out to wait behind the wheel
of the car.

As I sat there, Teresa began a series of trips from the house to the
car. She brought out clothes for the dry cleaner and put them in the
trunk. She brought out lunches for the children. Next she appeared
with Eric's car seat and put it in the car. Then she brought out Eric,
our preschooler, and put him in the car seat. Then she ushered out
our two daughters, and they joined me in the car. That morning I
watched Teresa make five or six trips from the house to the car, and
never once did it cross my mind, *Why don't you help her?* Rather,
the only thought on my mind was, *If she doesn't hurry up, I'm going
to honk the horn!*

Teresa describes that time in my life with one word: oblivious.
She used to say to me, "David, you are oblivious—a real space ca-
det with your head in the clouds. Your kids could be strangling
each other right before your eyes, and you would miss it." Teresa
was prone to exaggeration, so I thought her assessment was a tad
overstated.

Even in my hardheaded impatience that morning, I sensed I had blown it with my wife. When Teresa finally got into the car, I expected either World War III in my right ear or the Cold War for the next several days. And I deserved them both.

But that morning, a miracle took place: Teresa was patient and kind. God's Spirit was working in her life to help her make the right response to my oblivion that day. She didn't attack me or retreat into cold silence. Instead, as I drove, she talked about the two of us having lunch together that day. She mentioned special weekend plans. I thought I had forfeited all that with my insensitive behavior.

I had no defense for my wife's kind reply. Had she jumped all over me, I could have fought back with something like, "I did it because you nag me all the time." But she returned good for evil, so when I arrived at the church, I felt terribly guilty. I had good reason to feel that way because I *was* terribly guilty! And that's how I began my week as a minister who is supposed to lead and bless the people of God through obedience and example.

As I sat in my office that morning, God began to deal with me. The Holy Spirit seemed to say, "David, Teresa is right: you are oblivious to your wife, your children, and others around you. You are oblivious because you are self-centered. You are preoccupied with your own plans, your own goals, your own agenda, and your own ministry. And your self-centeredness has rendered you painfully insensitive to the very people you claim to love. Your selfishness is the reason you are married but still very much alone."

What was at the root of my self-centeredness? In a word, sin. Sin is the primary barrier between us, God, and others, robbing us of the intimacy God created us to enjoy. In Genesis 2, Adam was alone, and it was not good, so God provided Eve, and aloneness was removed. But in Genesis 3, Adam and Eve disobeyed God, and their relationship with him was broken. Sin also drove a wedge between Adam and Eve. The intimacy of their perfect relationship was marred by three roadblocks: *self-centeredness, self-reliance,* and *self-condemnation.*

I am thankful that God provided the ultimate remedy for sin. But from the Garden of Eden to the present, the sin that "so easily entangles us" (Heb. 12:1) is still a major roadblock to marriage intimacy. Sin is what keeps us alone—separated from God and others—in the face of Christ's invitation to be his colleague in removing aloneness.

SELF-CENTEREDNESS ROBS YOU AND
YOUR SPOUSE OF INTIMACY
My oblivious self-centeredness didn't change the fact that God cared for me. And it did not change the fact God wanted me to join him in loving ministry to Teresa. But my self-centeredness was robbing Teresa and me of God's specific blessing of intimacy in our marriage.

Underneath all self-centeredness is the fear that we won't receive what we want or need, so we tend to take from others selfishly. Chad was a taker. Whenever you saw him with his wife, Marsha, Chad dominated the conversation. Chad had a high need for attention, and he always did what he had to do to get it.

Marsha shared with Teresa and me what life was like with a taker: "When Chad comes home, all we talk about is *his* day—what went right for him, what went wrong for him, and everything in between. I used to try sharing about my activities, but I gave that up long ago. Chad is interested in only one thing, and that's Chad."

*S*IN *is the primary barrier between us, God, and others, robbing us of the intimacy God created us to enjoy.*

We suggested to Marsha that behind Chad's selfish taking was probably a little boy who is very afraid that he won't get the attention he craves. Marsha told us that when Chad was young, no one displayed interest in him or entered his world. His father seriously neglected him, and his mother was rarely around. So Chad began to demand attention rather than wait to receive it.

The problem with selfish taking is that it is never satisfied. Marsha related, "Chad seems to have an insatiable appetite for attention. No matter what I do or how much I give, it never seems to be enough. Chad always needs more."

Some may think that the logical solution to a spouse's self-centeredness is simply to deny what he or she keeps taking. For example, some would contend that when Chad demands Marsha's attention by talking only about himself and his day, she should just walk away and not listen. But even when someone inappropriately and selfishly takes, it is often still an attempt to fill a valid need. And denying a God-designed need is not the solution.

**The solution to self-centeredness is faith.** When self-centeredness expresses itself in impatient and selfish taking, it reflects a lack of faith. Self-centered spouses subconsciously doubt that God can or will provide what they need when they need it.

King David eventually realized that a lack of faith was at the root of his self-centered taking, expressed through his lust and adultery with Bathsheba and the deception that escalated to the murder of her husband, Uriah. God confronted David through the prophet Nathan, revealing that the king had despised or counted worthless God's provisions (see 2 Samuel 12:7-9). In response, David cried out, "I have sinned against the Lord" (2 Sam. 12:13). At the heart of the king's self-centered behavior was a lack of faith in God as his loving provider.

*WHEN self-centeredness expresses itself in impatient and selfish taking, it reflects a lack of faith.*

We must exercise our faith in a God who loves us so much that he will provide what we need through our relationship with him and through our spouse and others. How do we demonstrate such faith? Instead of taking, we practice giving without expecting a return. Chad is a good example. As Teresa and I talked with him and Marsha, he began to see his selfish taking as a lack of faith in God as his loving provider. So in faith, he began giving attention instead of taking it. It started small. When he arrived home from work, Chad would sit down with Marsha and ask her how her day went. He would ask each of his children what had happened in school that day. He deliberately gave of his time and interest to those he loved.

Both Marsha and Chad were amazed at the results. Marsha said, "I could tell the difference immediately. After I shared with Chad about my day, I sincerely wanted to know about his day. And when he talked, I was ready to listen and care—and he could sense that, which really met his need for my attention. Before, he was oblivious to what I shared, and I was too upset to care about what he shared. Now I think we are both receiving positive attention for the very first time."

In faith, Chad gave of himself, and in turn his need was met through his wife. The change didn't happen overnight, and Chad still struggles with the urge to take instead of give. But both Chad and Marsha are learning to become Christ's colleagues in the ministry of meeting each other's needs.

## SELF-RELIANCE ROBS YOU AND YOUR SPOUSE OF INTIMACY

An old gospel song summarizes the early years of my marriage to Teresa. The lyrics are, "He's all I need, he's all I need; Jesus is all I need." My skewed perspective of God, human needs, and relationships at the time convinced me that I needed only God in my life to have a successful marriage and fruitful ministry. My misunderstanding of God's design to remove my aloneness through him *and* Teresa fostered an unhealthy and unbiblical self-reliance that robbed our marriage of intimacy.

Furthermore, my attitude heaped condemnation on Teresa, communicating to her, "Ministry is my top priority, and it should be yours too. When are you going to grow up so you don't need so much of my personal time and attention?" One day, in my frustration to pressure Teresa to become as intense as I was about my ministry, I confronted her in the kitchen with an ultimatum: "Teresa, if you don't come along with me in serving God, I'm going on without you." Then I walked away.

Teresa explains her reaction to my statement:

"David's pointed words pierced me like a lance. He left me standing in the middle of the kitchen wondering exactly what he meant. Was he talking about leaving me *physically* through separation or divorce? Was he talking about giving up on me *spiritually* and *emotionally?* He could not have known the terrible pain those words caused me. And it only got worse.

"As David continued to lose himself in ministry, he *did* leave me every way except physically. I was alone and floundering while my husband filled his life with his top priority: the ministry. As a result, I became increasingly aloof and independent. I tried to play the 'ministry wife' role, but the more he pulled away into his work, the more I buried myself in activities at home with our children."

Teresa suffered tremendous self-doubt induced by the painful messages of my self-reliance. She often thought, *Maybe if I were more spiritual or sensed a deeper call to ministry, I wouldn't need David's love, acceptance, comfort, and encouragement so much. If I just had more of God, I wouldn't miss him so much when he is away doing ministry.*

I expected Teresa to deal with her needs in a self-reliant manner just as I did, and I chided her for not being spiritually independent. The more involved I became in the ministry, the more uncomfortable she became living in the fishbowl of congregational scrutiny.

Teresa explains, "As a fairly new Christian, I was still deciding what I believed and battling false guilt and self-condemnation over how insecure I felt in the ministry. Someone once made the thoughtless remark, 'I would never have believed you were David's wife since you're not as spiritual as he is.' But by this time I had developed a bubble of self-protection against the pain in my marriage and other relationships. I became extremely self-reliant in my own world in order to shut out the pain I experienced in my relationship with David and other Christians. I had mastered the skill of not feeling, not hurting. This was how I developed the numbness I later expressed when David asked, 'Teresa, do you really love me?'"

We had falsely equated self-reliance with spiritual maturity and emotional strength. As a result, our love for each other grew increasingly cold. To be sure, we needed to change our twisted view of God's design for marriage. But more than a renewed mind, we needed a humble heart.

**The solution to self-reliance is humility**. It is humbling for us to admit that we have needs we cannot meet on our own. And it is equally humbling to acknowledge that we are helpless to remove our aloneness apart from depending on God to minister to us and to involve other people in our lives as he desires. Hunkering down in a foxhole of self-reliance and just waiting to become more mature will not remove our aloneness. Maturity and strength in our relationships come only as we humbly depend on God to minister his grace to us, often through our spouse.

*W*E had falsely equated self-reliance with spiritual maturity and emotional strength.

Humility is not a single step of commitment or renewal that once and for all cancels out intimacy-robbing self-reliance. Humility is a heart attitude that is cultivated through the experiences that entice us to rely on ourselves. It is a daily process of becoming what Jesus called "poor in spirit" (Matt. 5:3). Humility grows as we say no to the temptation to meet our own needs without allowing God to involve others.

Not long ago, I again faced such a temptation. Our younger daughter, Robin, recently gave birth to our first grandchild, Zachary. Teresa and I were overjoyed with Robin and Ike, our son-in-law, at the new arrival. Of course, Teresa made room in her schedule to be available to Robin and little Zachary as much as possible. I watched Teresa with great fondness and admiration as she quickly became a doting grandmother. She beamed each time she held Zach. She loved pouring her affection on our little guy.

But as the days turned into weeks, I began to feel strangely uncomfortable around Zachary. Something "not good" was happening inside me. I would later come to identify this discomfort as fear. I was afraid that little Zach and other grandchildren to come would somehow rob me of some of Teresa's affection. In the early years of our marriage, Teresa had prioritized the children ahead of me, and it had been a source of conflict for us. That conflict had been healed long ago, but I now realized that the same fear was back in a new form.

How eager do you think I was to admit my fear and receive God's love through Teresa? My old self-reliance tempted me to keep quiet and tough it out. The thought went something like this: *Suck it up, Ferguson. You will look so immature and weak if you admit that little Zachary makes you feel insecure. Keep quiet and be a man, or say something and look childish—it's your choice.*

I have come to realize that admitting a weakness or sharing an area of personal need is not sign of weakness. That's a lie. Admitting weakness is a strength, and humility, though it may seem like weakness, is a great strength. So during a quiet moment alone with Teresa one day, I vulnerably confessed my fear of losing a measure of her affection, of losing my sense of being a priority to her. Her response was a clear indication of God's abundant grace. Her face broke into a warm, affectionate smile as she crossed the room to sit beside me on the couch. She pulled me close to her and said, "Honey, I love our dear Zachary very much. But a hundred Zacharys could never steal away the love I have for you."

We sat there holding each other with tears streaming down our faces. I also felt the arms of my heavenly Father wrapped around me, and I sensed his assurance that he and Teresa, his colleague in ministry, were committed to be there to fill my need to be a priority to Teresa. The result of God's work of humility in my heart in that situation was twofold: God was honored, and our marriage blessed.

*ADMITTING weakness is a strength, and humility, though it may seem like weakness, is a great strength.*

## SELF-CONDEMNATION ROBS YOU AND YOUR SPOUSE OF INTIMACY

A third barrier to intimacy in marriage is self-condemnation. Teresa shares an experience from her life:

"Self-condemnation is that often subtle but recurrent impression that you are not worth the love and care God desires to lavish on you through your spouse. This issue in my life had painfully hurt David and robbed our marriage of intimacy. No matter how much care and love David poured out to me, I could never fully receive it and appreciate it. No matter how deeply he grew to know me and become caringly involved in my life, my inner response was, *I don't deserve it.*

"The issue came to a head for me a few years ago on a trip to the United Kingdom. It seems that God does some of his deepest work in my life when we travel overseas. Maybe God catches me off guard and listening because I'm out of my environment and comfort zone. At least it seemed that way on this trip.

"David and I had just completed an extensive teaching and training tour in the United Kingdom. Leaving London, we headed for Gatwick Airport, about a ninety-minute drive, to fly home. David had allowed plenty of travel time to the airport, even in the traffic, so we had time for a brief stop. I was thirsty for a cold drink, but instead of asking David to stop for me, I said, 'Up ahead there's a petrol station where you can stop for a soft drink, if you would like one.' The way my request came out surprised even me.

"David's response, I would learn later, was calculated to lovingly challenge the self-condemnation that had stifled my joy for decades. He said, 'No thanks, I'm fine.' I sat there stunned, thinking, *But I would like a soft drink.* Then the Holy Spirit prompted the thought, *So what hinders you from asking David to stop for you?* I was still pondering the question when David broke the silence: 'But I'd love to stop and get *you* a drink, if *you* would like one.'

"Again I was silent. What was keeping me from saying yes? I knew David would stop if I wanted to. I was secure in his love and knew better than anyone that he has a giving heart. But tears began to flood my eyes and run down my cheeks as I contemplated the Spirit's next thought: *Aren't you worth David stopping just for you?*

"At that moment, David touched my shoulder and spoke four powerfully liberating words that answered the unspoken question. It was as if David's colleague in ministry to me, Jesus Christ, had also whispered the question to him. In response, David said to me, 'You're worth stopping for.' I began sobbing, suddenly flooded with gratitude for the love poured out to me. David's words, prompted by the compassionate heart of Christ, seemed to wash away years of childhood self-doubt and self-condemnation. My long-standing perception had been, *No one really wants to know me, so there must be something wrong with me. No one shows me attention, so it must be my fault. I'm just not worth being cared for.*

"This incident on the road to Gatwick Airport sparked for me a breakthrough that dominated our conversation for the rest of the trip home. I am finally breaking free of self-condemnation and able to express gratitude for David's love instead of discounting it out of feelings of unworthiness."

**The solution to self-condemnation is gratefulness.** It is nearly impossible to conquer self-condemnation through the mental gymnastics of trying to convince yourself that you are personally worthy of your spouse's love. Instead, when your spouse does something thoughtful for you, simply say something like "Thank you" or "I appreciate your love" or "I'm grateful to you and to God." Resist the temptation to qualify your appreciation by adding something like, "You really shouldn't have" or "I'm not worth the trouble." Expressing gratitude for your spouse's expressions of love, large or small, will free you to fully appreciate them. God will be glorified, and your relationship will be blessed.

## EMPOWERED TO BREAK DOWN BARRIERS

When the intimacy-robbing barriers of self-centeredness, self-reliance, and self-condemnation are broken down in your marriage, your aloneness is removed and you experience new levels of oneness. But how does it happen? Where do we find the faith, humility, and gratefulness necessary to surmount these debilitating barriers?

The answer is beautifully pictured for us in John 13, the narrative of Jesus gathering with his disciples in the Upper Room only hours before his arrest, trial, and crucifixion. Jesus and the Twelve are together to observe the Passover according to the Jewish tradition. But during the solemn meal, something very nontraditional occurs. Picture yourself in the room, reclined at the table with the disciples as the gripping events unfold.

*WHEN the intimacy-robbing barriers of self-centeredness, self-reliance, and self-condemnation are broken down in your marriage, your aloneness is removed and you experience new levels of oneness.*

Without a word, Jesus rises from the table, removes his outer garment, and wraps a towel around his waist. As he pours water into a basin, the disciples become curious. They whisper their concerns: "What is he doing? . . . Isn't that the servant's basin and towel? . . . Foot washing is a servant's job. . . . Surely he's not going to . . . " The room falls silent as Jesus brings the basin to the disciples one by one, unties their sandals, and gently cleanses their dusty, callused feet. Are you not amazed at the Master's expression of love for his disciples? He is only hours away from an agonizing death, and yet he spends precious minutes washing their dirty feet! These men must be very special to him.

But do the disciples deserve this loving touch? Are they as devoted to their Master as he is to them? No. There is some blatant self-centeredness in the room. Only moments ago "there arose also a dispute among [the disciples] as to which one of them was regarded to be greatest" (Luke 22:24). James and John, aptly called the Sons of Thunder, were in the middle of the storm as usual. They were always trying to grab the spotlight. The Master's heart is heavy with his impending suffering, and two of his closest friends are busy trying to assert their own importance.

But look. Jesus kneels before James and tenderly washes his feet. Then it's John's turn. The Master doesn't reprimand his disciples for their self-centeredness or lecture them on servanthood. He simply washes their feet. The pride and self-importance drain from their faces as they receive his compassionate ministry.

There is also self-reliance in the room. Jesus approaches Peter with the basin. "No, Lord," Peter protests, "you don't need to wash my feet." Unruffled by Peter's resistance, Jesus responds, "If I do not wash you, you have no part with Me" (John 13:8). Disarmed by the Master's love in the face of his own self-reliance, Peter backs off and eats humble pie: "Well, if washing is so important, then wash me all over, Lord, not just my feet!"

There is also self-condemnation in the room. Judas has already betrayed his Lord for thirty pieces of silver. He sits at the table under a cloud of guilt. His self-condemnation will soon drive him to take his own life. But look at this! There is Jesus, washing his betrayer's feet, extending the same compassion to him as to the others. What incredible love!

That's where freedom from self-centeredness, self-reliance, and self-condemnation begins. God's Spirit must lead us to the heart of the Savior as he encounters our sinful patterns of behavior. We must experience the wonder of a God who loves us and ministers to us despite our imperfection and failure. Once you begin to experience the miracle of what the apostle Paul called the constraining love of Christ (see 2 Corinthians 5:14, KJV), you will begin to walk free of the entangling sins that rob you and your spouse of intimacy.

## JESUS WASHES YOUR FEET: A MEDITATION

Can you see yourself there in the Upper Room with the Twelve? The constraining love of the Master is strong as he moves around the table washing the feet of each of his disciples. Then Jesus approaches you. He kneels down before you and gazes into your eyes. "Will you allow me to wash *your* feet?"

What will you say? Perhaps you are tempted to respond as self-centered James and John may have: "Lord, my feet are the least of my concerns. I have important needs to be met and problems to be solved. What are you going to do about them?"

Listen with your heart as Jesus lovingly responds: "Yes, I know all about your needs. I love you, and your concerns are my concerns. I will always be here to meet your needs right on time. You don't have to take; just receive. Will you, by faith, trust in my love, relax your grip on what you want, and allow me to meet your needs according to my will and schedule?"

Or do you find yourself resisting the foot washing in a self-reliant tone? "I appreciate the sentiment, Lord, but I can take care of myself. I may have needs, but I'll deal with them on my own terms."

Listen with your heart as Jesus lovingly responds: "Yes, you are very capable in many ways. But I did not create you with the capacity to fulfill all your own needs. You need me and others. Will you humbly submit to my love, give up your pride, and allow me to meet your needs through all the means at my disposal?"

Or perhaps you want to turn away from Jesus in shame and self-condemnation. "I can't let you wash my feet because I don't deserve it. I'm not worthy of your love."

Listen with your heart as Jesus lovingly responds: "Yes, I know about your hurts, your failures, and your scars. But I love you just as you are. If you were the only person on earth, I would go to the cross for you alone. Will you rejoice in my love and receive gratefully all that I have for you?"

With this poignant scene still fresh in your mind, we suggest that you take a moment to respond to the compassionate Christ who longs to minister to you despite your patterns of self-centeredness, self-reliance, or self-condemnation. Express your desire to trust him for meeting your needs, to humble yourself by allowing him to involve others in your life, and to respond gratefully as he lavishes his love on you.

As the constraining love of Christ releases you from old patterns of self-centeredness, self-reliance, or self-condemnation, you are better prepared to become his colleague in the ministry of deeply knowing and loving your spouse. As his Spirit empowers you to turn from yourself to the Savior, you become his effective instrument in removing your spouse's aloneness and nurturing intimacy in your relationship. And as you foster that intimacy through mutual faith, humility, and gratefulness, your marriage will be characterized by fulfilling oneness, and your oneness will bring joy and honor to the Creator.

PART
two

God's Companion
Our Needs Are Met

# CHAPTER 4

# Expressions of the Heart

As I drove out of the church parking lot and headed home—already thirty minutes late for supper—I thought, *It will be nice to spend a quiet evening at home.* It had been a long and emotionally draining day, and I was looking forward to a refreshing time with my family.

I was completely unaware of what Teresa's day had been like. The dog had chewed a hole in the arm of our relatively new couch. Eric had been sent home early from school for misbehavior. And every heating element in the range had burned out just as Teresa started fixing supper. It had not been a good day for her.

As I made my way through the garage toward the door into the house, I could hear Teresa giving our son a curt, drill-sergeant type command. When I entered the kitchen, I caught a glimpse of Eric shuffling out the front door. Teresa was slamming cupboard doors as she searched for a hot plate to prepare supper. She saw me out of the corner of her eye, but she said nothing. I figured that had something to do with my being over thirty minutes late. Tension was definitely in the air.

I set down my briefcase and watched my wife dart from one side of the kitchen to the other in a huff. Then I said, "What's wrong with you now?" It was more of an accusation than a question.

My comment was not received with warmth or appreciation, and by no means did it help the situation. But back in those days my input and advice rarely helped. In fact, whatever I said generally worsened the situation. And when on occasion Teresa did open up and unload what she was struggling with, I would often begin my response by saying something like "The reason I think that happened is . . ." or "I think it would help if you could just understand . . ." Messages like this only reinforced self-reliance in Teresa, implying, "You could solve your own problem without needing me if you would just get your act together."

Another one of my classic responses to Teresa's troubles was, "If you would just handle it my way next time, things will turn out much better." The message I was really communicating was, "If you weren't so stupid, you could do it right," reinforcing Teresa's self-condemnation. My pummeling her with advice only made things worse. Teresa lost all trust that I could help her, thereby reinforcing her self-reliance. No wonder there was a stifling desert of aloneness between us in those years. Instead of ministering with Christ to remove each other's self-centeredness, self-reliance, and self-condemnation, we were actively encouraging these intimacy-robbing patterns through our insensitive behavior.

## COMPANIONS IN THE MINISTRY OF MEETING NEEDS

Teresa and I had missed something vital during those years. We failed to understand that we have basic intimacy needs that each of us—in conjunction with Christ, our colleague—should meet in the other. Oh, I knew Teresa had needs, of course. She always seemed to need money for shopping. She needed me to be more consistent about getting home for supper on time, and she needed my help around the house. And I communicated my own list of "pressing needs." But we did not understand how God wanted to involve us in meeting each other's intimacy needs. And we did not realize that attending to these intimacy needs would remove our aloneness and deepen our relationship beyond measure.

There was another vital dimension of intimacy we had missed, and it related to our intimacy with Christ. God brought this dimension into sharp focus for me as I was meditating on Matthew 25:31-46. In this passage, Jesus tells a parable of the judgment, when the Son of Man will separate the people of the nations as a shepherd separates the sheep from the goats. To the righteous he will say, "Come, you who are blessed by my Father, inherit the Kingdom prepared for you from the foundation of the world. For I was hungry, and you fed me. I was thirsty, and you gave me a drink. I was a stranger, and you invited me into your home. I was naked, and you gave me clothing. I was sick, and you cared for me. I was in prison, and you visited me" (verses 34-36, NLT).

Of course, the righteous people in this judgment were not present during Christ's earthly ministry to care for him in these ways. They naturally respond, "Lord, when did we ever see you hungry and feed you? Or thirsty and give you something to drink? Or a stranger and show you hospitality? Or naked and give you clothing? When did we ever see you sick or in prison, and visit you?" (verses 37-39). The Son of Man explains, "I assure you, when you did it to one of the least of these my brothers and sisters, you were doing it to me!" (v. 40, NLT). The reverse image is presented in the dialogue with the unrighteous, who did *not* provide food, drink, shelter, and care. Christ explained, "I assure you, when you refused to help the least of these my brothers and sisters, you were refusing to help me." (v. 45, NLT).

The implications of this principle of "connectedness with Christ" in my actions were sobering and convicting as I thought about my marriage relationship.[1] When I withheld from Teresa my love, attention, care, and comfort, I was also withholding love, attention, care, and comfort from Christ. Whenever I hurt my wife through my self-centeredness and self-reliance, I also hurt my Sav-

[1]This principle of the mysterious connection with Christ is reinforced in many other passages, including Acts 22 and 1 Corinthians 12.

ior. Only the staggering, hopeful promise suggested in this parable rescued me from the utter despair of finding myself compared to the unrighteous. I sensed Christ saying to me, "When you love your wife, you love me. When you care for your wife, you care for me. When you bless your wife, you bless me. Just as I call you to minister to Teresa through me as my colleague, so I call you to minister to me through Teresa as my companion."

The answer to the question "What does God want out of our marriage?" is two-dimensional: horizontal and vertical. God is looking for a colleague in your marriage, one through whom he can love and nurture your spouse on the horizontal level. But he is also looking for a companion in your marriage through whom he will receive loving ministry. This is part of the marvelous mystery of intimacy. As you join with Christ to minister in your marriage, you remove not only your spouse's aloneness, you remove a measure of Christ's aloneness, who may have been loving your spouse without you. And in the process of ministering to your spouse, you not only become more intimate with him or her, you become more intimate with Christ, because what you do to your spouse, you do to him.

*I sensed Christ saying to me, "When you love your wife, you love me. When you care for your wife, you care for me. When you bless your wife, you bless me."*

In the previous section of this book we focused on the horizontal relationship of becoming Christ's *colleague* in your marriage. In this section we focus on the vertical relationship of becoming Christ's *companion* in your marriage.

## EXPERIENCING THE TRUTH RELATIONALLY

After fifteen years of marriage, Teresa and I both had a lot to learn about marriage intimacy. But learning was something I thought I did well. Jesus said, "Take My yoke upon you, and learn from Me"

(Matt. 11:29). For years I thought "learn from me" meant I should study the Bible, draw personal applications from its teachings, and proclaim those truths. I knew how to dissect a passage, gain insight from the Hebrew and Greek words, and exegete its meaning. And I had become proficient at declaring those meanings to Teresa through all my advice, counsel, and admonition. I knew quite well how to mine biblical truth and proclaim it to others.

But I was not *experiencing* the truth with Teresa. For all the *rational* truth I possessed about being a good Christian, husband, and father, I had overlooked the *relational* meaning of the truth. When we see truth only as something to proclaim and to defend rather than to experience, we diminish its value and it becomes irrelevant to us and those around us.

The day I accepted Christ's invitation to become his colleague in marriage, I began a journey of learning from him how to be a loving husband by experiencing his truth. Teresa embarked on a similar journey about that same time. It was only as we became yoked with Christ, who is relational truth personified, that we began to learn the truth experientially. And by experiencing the Bible with Teresa, I also became Christ's companion by ministering to his heart as I ministered to my wife.

*WHEN we see truth only as something to proclaim and to defend rather than to experience, we diminish its value and it becomes irrelevant to us and those around us.*

One of the first Bible passages I actually experienced in relationship with Teresa was another phrase in Matthew 11:29: "For I am gentle and humble in heart." The Lord challenged me with the goal of becoming a compassionate companion in ministering his love and care to Teresa.

It wasn't long until an opportunity arose to express his gentle and caring heart. I came home one evening and found Teresa angry over a string of frustrating events. Instead of my typical what's-wrong-with-you-now response, Proverbs 15:1 flooded my heart and mind: "A gentle answer turns away wrath." I came up next to Teresa, placed my hand on her shoulder, and said softly, "I can see that you're hurting, honey, and I just want you to know that I care."

A lightning bolt couldn't have shocked Teresa more. She turned abruptly to me, as if wondering if some stranger had walked into the room instead of me. Her next actions affirmed that my response had hit the target. Her shoulders relaxed and the frustration on her face drained away. Then she wrapped her arms around me and said in tears, "Oh David, you don't know how much I needed you today." She proceeded to tell me of her troublesome day, and I continued to be gentle. I provided no counsel, advice, or admonition. I didn't try to fix her problems right then. I just experienced Proverbs 15:1 by sharing my sincere, heartfelt, gentle words.

Teresa and I connected relationally that day, and her response was, "Thank you for caring, David. I love you." But there was something more. I caught a glimpse of the face of the Savior who, according to the mystery of our "connectedness with Christ," had received the ministry of gentleness as I experienced it with Teresa. My wife's trouble-filled day had sorrowed his heart too, and I sensed him saying to me as to a dear, loving friend, "Thank you for caring, David. I love you."

It wasn't only what I did—the gentle touch on the shoulder—or said—"I can see that you're hurting"—that met Teresa's need of the moment. She sensed that behind my loving touch and comforting words was a gentle heart that expressed, "I just want you to know that I care." I had begun learning gentleness from my colleague, who is gentle and humble in heart. And when I experienced Proverbs 15:1 relationally with Teresa, I sensed God's pleasure. He seemed to say to me, *When you experience my book in relationship with your wife, I am honored, and I will bless your marriage abundantly.*

Fostering intimacy in your marriage relationship isn't so much about *doing* loving deeds and *saying* loving words as it is about *being* loving persons who *do* loving things. Our doing should simply reflect our loving. Our doing should be the expression of our caring involvement. And God's Word is quite specific about what caring involvement looks like. Scripture identifies how God has expressed his love toward us and how we are to love others in return. That day with Teresa, I experienced the gentle heart of the Savior and responded with a gentle touch and word. As we experienced that passage together, an intimacy need was met.

*F*OSTERING *intimacy in your marriage relationship isn't so much about doing loving deeds and saying loving words as it is about being loving persons who do loving things.*

How do we determine valid intimacy needs that we are to meet in one another by experiencing Bible verses? In Scripture, whenever you find God demonstrating his love for his human creation, he is identifying a valid intimacy need he desires to meet, first for us and then through us to others. For example, Romans 15:7 says, "Accept each other just as Christ has accepted you; then God will be glorified" (NLT). Since Christ accepted us, we must have a need for acceptance. Therefore we are to *be* accepting and *convey* acceptance to our spouses.

Scripture identifies a number of other intimacy needs, such as our need for comfort, attention, appreciation, support, encouragement, affection, respect, security, and approval, and we will discuss these needs thoroughly in the next chapter. In each case, we are to abundantly receive them from Christ, our colleague, who embodies all of these qualities. Then we are to experience these qualities through his Word with our spouses and minister to Christ, our companion. We find this two-directional, need-meeting ministry in 1 Peter 4:10: "As each one has received a special gift, employ it in serving one another, as good stewards of the manifold grace of

God." As we freely receive God's multifaceted grace to meet our needs, we are encouraged to freely give of this grace to others. Has God accepted us? Absolutely. Having experienced his gift of acceptance, we are then to minister acceptance to our spouses. Has God been affectionate toward us? Has he provided needed security? Has he encouraged our hearts? Of course, and he continues to pour out his multifaceted grace to us. As God meets these needs in our lives, we are challenged to meet these needs in the lives of those around us, beginning at home.

Many people think of meeting biblically valid intimacy needs in their spouses as merely something else to add to their daily to-do list. And when they do something good, they think, *There, I can check that one off my list.* Following through on certain behaviors and responses is important, but "doing for" does not fully meet the need if "being with" is not also the priority.

### "BEING WITH" EMPOWERS "DOING FOR"

When Meg and Tom, a young Christian couple, came to Teresa and me for help, Meg complained that she sensed distance between them. She felt somewhat disconnected from Tom. "I know Tom loves me because he does so many things for me," she said. "But I still don't feel as close to him as I think I could."

I turned to Tom and asked him what he thought about Meg's comment. "Well, I've never been a touchy-feely kind of guy," he explained to us. "I love Meg, and I do a lot of things to prove it. I don't really know what else I can do."

"I'm not complaining about what you do for me, Tom," Meg interrupted. "In fact, you probably do *too* much for me. That's not the point."

Tom looked at me and shrugged as if to say, "I guess I don't get the point."

I turned to Meg. "I sense that Tom is a good provider, that he's always there to give you what you need materially."

Meg nodded, adding, "He's good about helping around the house and being involved with our kids. And he always remembers to give me cards or gifts on special occasions. As I said, he's doing the right things, but I just don't feel close to him."

I went on. "Then perhaps you need to know more about how to *be with* each other emotionally. If it's okay with you, I would like you to experience a Scripture passage together." The couple agreed.

I directed their attention to the first phrase of Romans 12:15: "Rejoice with those who rejoice." Then I asked Tom to think of a pleasant memory from his past and share it with Meg. I asked Meg to be ready to rejoice with Tom, that is, to express her joy at Tom's happy experience. After a little prompting, Tom told about the boyhood thrill of receiving his first bicycle. Meg's response was warm and enthusiastic: "I'm so happy you had that experience. I can just see a little boy named Tommy riding proudly around the neighborhood on his new bike."

Then I asked Meg to tell about a happy memory so Tom could rejoice with her. She shared that, as the only girl with four brothers, she rarely got to do things with her father. But one day when Meg was ten years old, her dad took her to the park alone, and they spent hours walking and talking and feeding the squirrels. She concluded, "That outing with my dad was very meaningful and precious to me."

Teresa, who was sitting near Meg, couldn't contain herself. She touched Meg's hand and said with tears of joy, "Oh, Meg, I am so happy that you had that wonderful day with your daddy."

I looked over at Tom and nodded, encouraging him to join in. He cleared his throat and spoke in a deliberate and matter-of-fact tone. "Well, that's good, Meg. You know, you were probably happy because your father was such a busy man. When he took time with you, it made you feel special. What do you think?"

Meg stared at Tom for several silent seconds, then she turned to Teresa and me. "Do you see what I mean?"

I believe Tom was sincere, but he was clueless about "being with" his wife in her happiness. Instead of rejoicing with Meg, he analyzed her experience intellectually. Instead of joining his wife in her joyful emotions, he remained in his rational, logical world. Tom knew how to *do* things *for* his wife, and this is important and necessary. But because he did not allow himself to *be with* Meg emotionally, her need for deep intimacy went unmet—and she was often alone.

MAKING THE EMOTIONAL CONNECTION

Intimacy in a marriage relationship develops as we invest ourselves in being *with* each other on a deep personal level. Jesus modeled this vital relational principle during his earthly ministry. Notice how he selected his disciples: "He appointed twelve, that *they might be with Him,* and that He might send them out to preach, and to have authority to cast out the demons" (Mark 3:14-15, emphasis added). The New Living Translation rendering of this verse includes these words: "Then he selected twelve of them to be his regular companions, calling them apostles" (v. 14, NLT). He sent them out to preach, and he gave them authority to cast out demons. There was a lot of *doing* in store for Christ and his disciples over the next three years— preaching, teaching, and battling the forces of darkness. But Christ's first concern in choosing ministry assistants was having companions, people to *be with.* He sought out a small band of men who could share both the joys and trials of ministry life. Among these men Jesus would invite three—Peter, James, and John—to share with him the high joy of the Transfiguration (see Mark 9:2-8) and the deep sorrow of Gethsemane (see Matthew 26:36-46).

In God's design for marriage, a husband and wife grow in oneness by being with each other emotionally through all of life's experience. Day-to-day life is often like a wild roller-coaster ride. We have the ups and downs of good times and bad, triumph and tragedy, health and sickness, pleasure and pain—and everything in between. Along with the variety of life experiences, we ride through a broad range of emotions: joy, disappointment, anger, sadness, exhilaration, embarrassment, shame, ecstasy, loneliness, despair. Christ, your companion in marriage, calls you to join him in *being with* your spouse emotionally through everything life throws at you. And as you minister to your spouse's need for emotional closeness, you are also ministering to Christ, who knows the fulfillment of being with loving companions.

Being with your spouse means you are there to acknowledge and share whatever emotions he or she may experience. For example, your husband comes home from a service club meeting and announces that he was chosen member of the year. He beams with pride as he displays the beautiful plaque with his name engraved on it. Being with him at this moment may sound something like this: "Honey, I'm so happy for you. Your plaque is beautiful. I'm so thrilled for you that you were honored in this way." You may be eager to help him find a place to display his plaque (and to make sure he doesn't hang it in your dining room). But let the *doing* follow the *being* of experiencing his joy with him.

*INTIMACY in a marriage relationship develops as we invest ourselves in being with each other on a deep personal level.*

Or let's say that your wife calls you to report that she has just had a blowout on the freeway and nearly lost control of the car. She is obviously shaken. Being with her at this moment may sound something like this: "I can tell that you're really upset, sweetheart, and I'm so sad that this happened to you." You may be concerned with the *doing* of making sure she gets home safely and getting the tire changed. You may be dying to ask her what caused the blowout and if the car was damaged. But *being with* your spouse emotionally in these moments provides the connection that empowers meaningful *doing*. Without the shared *being*, even well-intentioned *doing* may leave your spouse alone and vulnerable.

Recently, a minister told us in sadness that his wife was having an affair with a divorced man. It turns out that his wife met this man at the field where the couple's twelve-year-old daughter played her soccer matches. The minister was seemingly too busy with church activities to attend the matches, so his wife attended without him and cheered their daughter on. Also in the bleachers at every game was the single father of another girl on the team. The team was undefeated, so the two parents shared the common excitement of their daughters' success. The emotional camaraderie pulled them together and met their unmet needs for intimacy, leaving them vulnerable to some wrong choices.

We do not believe that every illicit affair is the result of a husband and wife failing to be with each other emotionally. But when you identify emotionally with your spouse in both the positive and painful experiences of life, the two of you will develop a closeness that leads to intimacy. And intimacy provides great protection against temptation.

A friend of ours recently remarked that rejoicing with his wife in good times was a positive and uplifting exercise for him, but he struggled to identify with her painful emotions. We encouraged him that the inevitable disappointments and pains in life provide excellent opportunities to develop an intimate relationship with his wife.

It is the case for all of us. "Weeping with those who weep" is about being compassionate and sympathetic with your spouse (see Romans 12:15; Hebrews 10:34; 1 Peter 3:8). It's about identifying with your dear one's hurt and communicating that you care. When someone is *with us* during our trials by sharing our feelings, a very positive result occurs: We connect emotionally, we experience love, and we feel less alone.

## SHARING FROM A LOVING HEART

Intimacy is not a product of facts, logic, or reason; it is the outflow of a loving heart. Sometimes we make this idea of relating to each other on an emotional level too complicated. In reality, connecting emotionally is a matter of letting compassion flow in the normal, daily ups and downs of life together.

A beautiful example is found in John 11. Jesus was good friends with a man named Lazarus and his two sisters, Mary and Martha. After Lazarus's death in Bethany, Jesus came to visit Mary and Martha. When Mary, in tears over her brother's death, greeted the Lord, he also wept. It was the natural outflow of his heart, identifying with Mary in her sorrow, sharing her grief. The image was so powerful that even the unbelieving Jews looking on commented about the love being demonstrated (see verses 33-36).

*INTIMACY is not a product of facts, logic, or reason; it is the outflow of a loving heart.*

Connecting emotionally is so basic that even a child can understand it. One of our coworker couples has a four-year-old granddaughter named Mattie. Grandpa and Grandma love to have Mattie visit and spend the night, and during one such visit, Grandma announced that it was bedtime. Mattie was having such a good time playing that her face clouded over with disappointment. Grandma pulled little Mattie up on her lap and said, "I know you are so disappointed. I think you need some comfort." Grandma held Mattie for several minutes and shared gentle, comforting words that identified with Mattie's disappointment. Mattie soon settled down and got ready for bed without complaint.

Weeks later, Mattie and her mother, Joyce, stopped by to see Grandma. "Mom, a few days ago Mattie was struggling over some minor disappointment," Joyce said during the visit. "She turned to me and said, 'Mommy, I think I need some comfort.' I asked Mattie what she meant, and she said that Grandma gave her comfort and it helped. So she wondered if I could do it too. What was she talking about?"

Grandma turned to her granddaughter. "Mattie, show me what comfort looks like." Little Mattie slipped over to her grandma and hugged her tenderly. Then Grandma said, "Mattie, what does comfort sound like?" Still holding her grandma affectionately, Mattie said, "It sounds like, 'I'm sorry you're sad.' "

Compassion isn't complicated. Even a small child can grasp its purity and simplicity because it comes from the heart, not from the intellect.

Tom approached his life with Meg "head first" instead of "heart first." That's why Meg didn't feel as if they were connecting. When Meg shared the fond memory of a time with her father in the park, she didn't need to have it analyzed. She needed Tom to be with her in that memory by entering into her excitement with her.

Later in our discussion with the couple, Tom was able to reflect on another memory, and this one was both happy and sad. "When I graduated from college, I was the first one in my entire family ever to do so. I was so proud of my feat, and I thought they would be too. But nobody celebrated my graduation. No party, no cards, no gifts—nothing."

Hearing the story for the first time, Meg began to cry, first in sadness. "Honey, I'm so sorry no one celebrated your accomplishment with you," she said as tears streamed down her face. "I'm so sad for you that your special day went unnoticed." Then her tears turned to joy. "But it's so wonderful that you reached your goal. I'm so happy for you that you had the joy of receiving your degree."

Meg's compassionate response was a clear picture to Tom of how he needed to be with her through life's joys and trials.

Being with your spouse during happy and joyful times means sharing your good feelings about those experiences. It means identifying with your partner's joy, sharing a hug, a kiss, or a high five, and saying something like, "That's wonderful! I'm so glad that happened. I'm excited and pleased for you."

Sharing your spouse's tough times might include a comforting embrace, sympathetic tears, or a sigh of grief. Your compassion may be expressed in gentle words from the heart, something like, "I am so very sorry. I'm here for you. I'll go through this with you. How I love you."

Virtually every experience of daily life is an opportunity to connect emotionally with your spouse. Identifying with each other's joys and trials—small or great—by experiencing Romans 12:15—rejoicing with those who rejoice and weeping with those who weep—on a daily basis will deepen your intimacy. And consider what goes on in heaven as you care for each other in this way. Imagine a couple of angels looking down on you as you rejoice with one another and weep with one another. "What are they doing?" asks one. The other answers, "It looks like Romans 12:15 to me!" And God is there too, beaming with pleasure as he sees you experiencing his book.

*VIRTUALLY every experience of daily life is an opportunity to connect emotionally with your spouse.*

Learning to be with your spouse and identify with him or her emotionally goes far beyond Romans 12:15. There are many more Bible passages to be experienced in the ongoing process of deepening your oneness as a couple. In fact, there is at least one Scripture passage you can experience that will help meet each of our intimacy needs. In the next chapter we will focus on ten intimacy needs and how you can meet them.

# CHAPTER 5

# Meeting the Need of the Moment

At the ripe old age of sixteen, I was already married and out of high school, having graduated early. I had two jobs and was a full-time student at a community college. Even with all my adult responsibilities, I still had a lot of growing up to do. My grandfather was a key person to point me in the right direction. Here's an example.

Between our home in Pampa, Texas, and the community college I attended lay about thirty miles of open highway. Juggling a marriage, two jobs, and schoolwork, my time was at a premium. So I figured I could save five minutes to and from school each day if I drove 80 mph on Highway 152 instead of staying within the 55 mph speed limit.

But I had a problem. The Highway Patrol occasionally monitored Highway 152, and I was getting pulled over for speeding every month or so. Teresa told me I was foolish to speed like that, and my parents begged me to slow down. But this only fueled my rebellious spirit into trying to beat the speed trap. As a rebel and an unbeliever, I tried everything I could think of to avoid detection. But I soon got to the point that I would lose my license if I were to be stopped for speeding one more time.

Granddad was a wise old man, and I liked him a lot. One Sunday afternoon he pulled me aside for a man-to-man chat. He said, "David, I hear that the law's been nailing you for speeding and that you're about to lose your license." I acknowledged his information with a nod. He continued, "Well, you know something? I think they've marked your car. I think the cops know you drive Highway 152 every day, and they're just waiting to hammer you."

As I surveyed Granddad's face, I sensed he had a plan. "You got an idea, Granddad?" I asked.

"Sure do," he replied. "I'll loan you my truck, and they'll never know it's you."

I was sure I had found a kindred spirit. Granddad seemed to understand me. I eagerly agreed to his plan, and we walked to the shed with arms around each other's shoulders to get Granddad's truck.

The next morning I made my way toward Highway 152, excited about putting one over on the law. As I turned onto the open road, I roared through the gears to get the old truck up to my customary speed. But when the speedometer reached about 55 mph, it stopped moving, even though my foot was still pressing the accelerator to the floorboard.

I was puzzled for a moment, then a smile broke over my face, and soon I was laughing out loud. Wise old Granddad had put one over on *me*. He knew all the time that his truck wouldn't go faster than 55. That was why he talked me into driving it. So I drove Granddad's truck for the rest of the term and didn't get one more citation. More important, the incident deepened my relationship with Granddad, and he became a powerful influence in my life for good.

What was it about Granddad that prompted change in my life where others had failed? Cajoling and hounding from my wife and parents had only encouraged the rebel in me. And the law's threat to revoke my license had not slowed me down. What had Granddad provided that the others had not?

Granddad met a need in my life that even the well-intentioned efforts of other family members had not met. I needed someone to love me and be with me even in my rebellion and failure. I needed acceptance, and Granddad accepted me, rebellion and all. He cared enough about me to know me and accept me for who I was without enabling or encouraging my wrong behavior. His example of acknowledging and meeting my deep need would later help influence the turnaround in my relationship with Teresa and in my relationship with God. Granddad modeled for me the relational benefits of meeting intimacy needs. When I became a Christian a few years later, I realized that the Spirit had used my granddad's acceptance to help me see God's character better.

## MEETING NEEDS MOMENT BY MOMENT

Loving your spouse involves being with that person during the full range of his or her life experiences. It is during these experiences that God wants to involve you in meeting your spouse's intimacy needs. The apostle Paul instructs us to offer words of edification "according to the need of the moment, that it may give grace to those who hear" (Eph. 4:29). Notice two vital truths about needs in this passage. First, it is important to understand the "need of the moment" before speaking or acting. This means you must discern what your spouse is going through at the moment and what intimacy needs are going unmet. Second, you have the awesome potential and privilege to "give grace" as you respond to your spouse's need. Remember: Your wise colleague in ministry is always there to teach you and help you, and your loving companion is honored and blessed as you minister to him through your spouse.

*LOVING your spouse involves being with that person during the full range of his or her life experiences.*

In the following pages we will explore ten intimacy needs that appear to be among the most significant in Scripture:

1. Comfort
2. Attention
3. Acceptance

4. Appreciation
5. Support
6. Encouragement
7. Affection
8. Respect
9. Security
10. Approval

Does everyone have all these needs? Yes, to some degree. But due to a variety of factors, each of us seems to have a few needs that are a higher priority than the others. For example, my top three intimacy needs are respect, affection, and comfort; Teresa's are attention, security, and acceptance. Determining the top three or four needs for you and your spouse will prove extremely valuable to your ministry of caring involvement to each other.

This list of needs is by no means comprehensive, but it will provide an excellent starting point to help you learn to identify and meet intimacy needs in your spouse. The Intimacy Needs Assessment Inventory in appendix A will help you and your spouse identify your top needs.

### 1. Comfort: Easing Your Partner's Grief or Pain

Life is full of negative and hurtful experiences: disappointments, losses, relational conflict and rejection, physical and emotional pain, etc. When your spouse has suffered some kind of painful experience, his or her need of the moment is for comfort. To comfort someone means to ease the grief or pain and to provide strength and hope to go on. When you comfort your spouse, you are experiencing 2 Corinthians 1:3-4: "Blessed be the God and Father of our Lord Jesus Christ, the Father of mercies and God of all comfort; who comforts us in all our affliction so that we may be able to comfort those who are in any affliction with the comfort with which we ourselves are comforted by God."

When your spouse is hurting in some way, comfort means identifying with that hurt and compassionately communicating your sorrow and concern. The "gentle word" God prompted me to share with Teresa at the end of her bad day was an expression of comfort: "I can see that you're hurting, honey, and I just want you to know that I care." It met the need of the moment, and we experienced deeper intimacy as a result. And my companion Jesus, who was hurting with Teresa, was comforted and blessed.

Meeting the need for comfort is not about trying to "fix" your spouse, solve his or her problems, or even offer helpful advice. It is not about correcting behavior or sharing a motivational pep talk. Such efforts may help at times, but they do not bring comfort. Romans 12:15 instructs us first to weep with those who weep to meet the need of the moment. Any needed fixing, counsel, or helpful assistance can come later.

Kevin was a fixer. For nearly thirty years of marriage, his response to all of Penny's problems was to fix them. When a household appliance broke, Kevin had it fixed in order to make Penny's work easier. If they faced a budget crisis, Kevin diligently worked the numbers and found the money, meeting Penny's need for financial security. Penny deeply appreciated her husband's commitment to provide for her. But Penny had one need that Kevin could not meet by fixing something.

Penny's childhood memories were a dark, painful gray. She had been physically and emotionally abused by a father who did not know how to express love. As a result, Penny's scrapbook of photos from her unhappy growing-up years portrayed her with a glum expression. Only one snapshot, taken at about age three, captured a glimmer of girlish excitement. Her father's abuse had stifled sweet little Penny and robbed her of a joyful childhood.

*W*HEN *your spouse is hurting in some way, comfort means identifying with that hurt and compassionately communicating your sorrow and concern.*

Penny's buried hurt resurfaced every time she and Kevin visited her parents. Driving home from these painful encounters, Penny was often depressed. True to his nature, Kevin moved in to fix it. "You don't have to feel this way," he would say sternly. "Don't let him jerk you around by your emotions. See your father for the emotionally hurting man that he is, and forgive him." But the more Kevin tried to fix the problem, the more Penny hurt. And the more Penny hurt, the more frustrated and inadequate Kevin felt about not being able to help her resolve her childhood pain.

Kevin and Penny attended one of our conferences for ministry couples. During an exercise in experiencing biblical truth, this pair had difficulty. When I dismissed participants to their hotel rooms, I urged couples to share with each other a painful, disappointing, or sad memory—a death in the family, a financial disaster, a failed relationship, etc. Then I encouraged them to experience Romans 12:15 by compassionately mourning those hurts with each other. I said it could be as simple as saying something like, "I'm saddened by what you experienced. Because I love you, I'm so sorry you had to go through that pain."

But Kevin was apprehensive. He explained to me later, "To be honest, David, I just couldn't see how feeling sad with someone would be that much help. So I suggested to Penny that we put off the exercise until we went home after the conference. Then I assured her, 'I really do want to feel with you about your past. Because when I think of that picture of you as a happy, excited three-year-old, I really feel . . .' All of a sudden an overwhelming sense of sadness came over me for that little girl who had lost her excitement and joy. Tears welled up in my eyes. When I looked over at Penny, she was sobbing.

"I pulled Penny to my lap and wrapped my arms around her. I really began to feel her pain. I said, 'I'm so sorry you had to hurt like that.' Tears flooded my eyes. 'I'm so sorry for that little girl, for all that she suffered.' Then I could say no more. We sobbed in each other's arms for several minutes. For the first time in thirty years of marriage I had met my wife's need for comfort. I never knew what Penny needed from me, and Penny didn't even know exactly what she needed from me. But when I began to hurt with my wife, it somehow enabled her to begin to release the pain and find additional freedom from the hurt."

A significant measure of Penny's aloneness was removed when she and Kevin experienced God's Word together. The result was a greater sense of intimacy between them. And Kevin became more attuned to Penny's need for comfort from both past and present hurts.

**What might the need for comfort sound like?** A spouse in need of comfort is saying in effect, "When I'm hurting, don't try to analyze the situation, fix the problem, or give me a pep talk. Just hold me, let me feel sad, and feel sad with me. Gently reassure me that you care that I am hurting and that you love me."

**What might comfort sound like?** The words of comfort may include: "I'm saddened that this happened to you"; "This must be very difficult for you"; "I hurt for you right now"; "I'm here if you need someone to listen or hold your hand"; "I love you"; "I am committed to help you through this tough time"; "I'm so sorry."

**What might comfort look like?** Comfort may appear as a tender embrace, sitting together quietly while holding hands, or shared tears. Comfort may include any compassionate physical expression that reflects your spouse's pain.

## 2. Attention: Taking Thought of Your Partner

We were all born with a need for others to notice us, be interested in us, and care for us. Yet we live in a hectic me-first culture. People everywhere seem focused on their own agendas, priorities, careers, interests, and activities. This self-centered focus often extends into a marriage. You and your spouse likely have different jobs, different hobbies, different ministries in your church, and even a different circle of friends. As such, it is easy for either or both of you to feel ignored, overlooked, unimportant, and unloved in your marriage. When this becomes evident, attention is the need of the moment.

Meeting your spouse's need for attention means that you take thought of him or her and convey appropriate care, interest, and concern. It means caring enough to enter your partner's world, learn what is important to him or her, and become involved in your partner's life. When you meet each other's need for attention, you are experiencing God's Word as expressed in 1 Corinthians 12:25: "This makes for harmony among the members, so that all the members care for each other equally" (NLT). And when you give this caring attention to your spouse, you are giving attention to Christ.

**What might the need for attention sound like?** If your spouse could verbalize this feeling, he or she might say, "I'm eager for you to take thought of me and enter my world—to show an interest in what I do and what I like, to care about my dreams and aspirations. But don't show me attention just because I want you to, but because you want to, because you truly care about me."

**What might attention sound like?** "I will enter your world and get to know you because I care for you"; "Tell me about your day"; "I want to know how you feel about your latest project"; "What are your hopes for the holiday season?"; "Tell me about your dreams and goals"; "What would you like to do tonight?"; "Anything that is important to you is important to me."

**What might attention look like?** You demonstrate attention when you set aside your own interests for a time and focus on doing what your spouse wants to do or say. This may take the form of asking your spouse about his or her day and listening with interest. It may mean that you sit down to watch your partner's favorite TV program together or suggest that the two of you make the rounds of the garage sales because that's what your partner likes to do on a free morning. It may mean taking a class together because it is something your partner always wanted to do. Attention may mean leisurely sipping coffee together while you ask your spouse about his or her dreams for a family vacation or a career change.

### 3. Acceptance: Receiving Your Partner in Spite of Faults

We all have the need for others to accept us for who we are, "warts and all." When we accept one another as spouses, we are experiencing Romans 15:7: "Accept each other just as Christ has accepted you; then God will be glorified" (NLT). Genuine acceptance is able to separate the person from his or her behavior, just as Christ loved and accepted us in spite of our sin.

As a sixteen-year-old kid, my need of the moment was for someone to look past my youthful rebellion and recklessness and *love* me anyway. Granddad accepted me without condoning my behavior, and his accepting love helped form a strong and lasting bond between us.

**What might the need for acceptance sound like?** At its core, your partner's need for acceptance may sound something like this: "Please allow me to make mistakes, and love me anyway. I know I'm not perfect, but I need you to look beyond my failures and imperfection and love me for who I am. I always need ten times more positive feedback than constructive criticism."

**What might acceptance sound like?** When your partner does something different from how you would do it or makes a costly mistake or gets into a fender bender, acceptance will focus on the person you love, not the difference or failure: "Even if

*G*ENUINE *acceptance is able to separate the person from his or her behavior, just as Christ loved and accepted us in spite of our sin.*

nothing about you changed, I would love you anyway, just the way you are"; "I want to know how you're feeling, because how you feel is important to me"; "I'm so proud of how you handled that situation"; "What happened to the car doesn't matter to me; I'm just glad you're all right, because you matter to me."

**What might acceptance look like?** After a disagreement or a clash of wills, your acceptance might take the form of fixing your partner a favorite meal, sending a bouquet of flowers, initiating a romantic interlude, or any outward expression that communicates, "We may not always see eye to eye, but I always love you."

### 4. Appreciation: Communicating Gratefulness and Praise to Your Partner

We all need to sense that others not only recognize who we are and what we have done but also appreciate and praise our efforts. When you express appreciation to your spouse, you are experiencing Paul's commendation in 1 Corinthians 11:2: "I praise you because you remember me in everything, and hold firmly to the traditions." Meeting the need for verbalized praise and loving appreciation in your partner will deepen the intimacy of your relationship. And as you appreciate your spouse, you are appreciating your dear colleague and companion, Jesus Christ.

**What might the need for appreciation sound like?** Whether or not your spouse has verbalized it to you, his or her need for appreciation might sound something like this: "Please let me know when you appreciate what I do for you, even the little things that can be overlooked or taken for granted. I need to sense your appreciation in tangible ways. Your praise is especially meaningful when you share it in front of others, such as our children, family members, and friends."

**What might appreciation sound like?** "Kids, your mom is very special. I'm so glad that she is my wife and best friend"; "Thank you for the delicious meal"; "I see that you cleaned out the garage, and I really appreciate it"; "Thank you for your thoughtfulness. I am so grateful that you called"; "You always remember to open doors for me, and it makes me feel so special"; "I'm so grateful for your cheery attitude and positive outlook."

**What might appreciation look like?** Verbalized praise can be shared in sticky notes left in conspicuous places like a bathroom mirror, the refrigerator door, the car steering wheel, or inside the morning newspaper. Thoughtful words of appreciation can be communicated in ways such as greeting cards, letters, and E-mail. Nonverbal praise may take the form of an enthusiastic hug, a specially chosen gift, or a surprise date.

### 5. Support: Helping to Carry Your Partner's Burden

When water beds were just coming into vogue, Teresa and I wanted to see what they were all about. It so happened that a college student in our ministry had a king-size water bed he couldn't use, so we volunteered to store it for him—if he would let us use it. He agreed. We set up the bed in our bedroom and filled it with water. But it didn't take long to realize that we hated sleeping on a water bed. So I took on the challenge of getting the bed out of our room.

I knew nothing about emptying a water bed, but my idea was to drag the mattress full of water to the bedroom window and somehow pour out the water. So I rolled the mattress—which seemed to weigh a ton—onto the floor. As I was trying to drag this bag full of water to the window, Teresa was standing at a distance giving advice: "Pull it up there . . . now move it over here . . . now grab that other end." In the meantime, my frustration was rising into the red zone because I could not make the mattress go where I wanted it to go. Finally, I said, "Teresa, stop telling me what to do; come over here and help me do it!"

Our experience with the water bed is a

*MEETING the need for verbalized praise and loving appreciation in your partner will deepen the intimacy of your relationship.*

89

good example of what support is not. Support is not something you can do from a distance. Support means coming alongside your spouse and lending your shoulder to share the weight of a burden or struggle. The burden could be physical or material, such as moving furniture, addressing Christmas cards, planting or tending a garden. But burdens can also be relational or emotional, such as disciplining a child, making a financial decision, or dealing with a difficult relative, friend, or neighbor. When you lend your support to your partner, you are experiencing Galatians 6:2: "Bear one another's burdens, and thus fulfill the law of Christ."

*Support means coming alongside your spouse and lending your shoulder to share the weight of a burden or struggle.*

**What might the need for support sound like?** When your spouse is struggling under a heavy load, he or she may want to communicate: "I need to know that you are available to help me in this situation—and that you really want to help me. The last thing I need when I'm overburdened or stressed out is a lecture."

**What might support sound like?** Words like these help convey your readiness to provide support: "I sense you can use some help. Please allow me to carry some of the load"; "Is there anything I can do to help you today?"; "If you show me what you need done, I'll be glad to help"; "I'm here for you and I'll go through this with you"; "Tell me what's wrong; maybe I can help"; "I know you're struggling, so let me pray for you."

**What might support look like?** Support may be demonstrated by helping your spouse complete a chore, finish a project, prepare for or clean up after an event, build or repair something. Perhaps you might take on household duties for a weekend so your spouse can attend a retreat. Support may take the form of offering to listen compassionately as your spouse talks through a problem, concern, or fear and then of assisting in a solution or response.

**6. Encouragement: Urging or Inspiring Your Partner toward a Goal**
Everybody gets discouraged at times, particularly when we lose sight of a goal or lose hope through disappointment, frustration, rejection, or failure. In your spouse's moments of discouragement, the need of the moment is for encouragement. As you encourage your partner, you supply the needed motivation to go on and inspire courage, spirit, and hope. And you are experiencing Hebrews 10:24-25: "Let us consider how to stimulate one another to love and good deeds, . . . encouraging one another."

*IN your spouse's moments of discouragement, the need of the moment is for encouragement.*

What might the need for encouragement sound like? "When I feel discouraged or disappointed, I need you to assure me that everything is all right and help me get back on track. I need you to lift my spirits and share your confidence that I can still reach my goals. You encourage me by helping me see the light at the end of the tunnel."

What might encouragement sound like? "I know this is a difficult time for you, but I believe in you"; "What can I do to help you accomplish your goals this week?"; "So many people are going to be affected by your good work on this project. I know you will finish it successfully"; "If anyone can make it, you can"; "Tomorrow is a new day, and I am excited to experience it with you."

What might encouragement look like? When your spouse is feeling down, your encouragement may be shared in the form of a reassuring smile, a cold glass of lemonade, or a cheery note. Being available to spend time praying with your spouse, discussing his or her options, or just being together silently may provide encouragement. Or it might help to offer an uplifting diversion, such as dinner out, a drive in the country, or a get-together with friends to play games or pray together.

## 7. Affection: Demonstrating Care through Loving Touch and Affirming Words

We were created with the capacity and need to receive love and care through affectionate touch and loving words. When you share affectionately with your spouse, you are experiencing Romans 16:16: "Greet one another with a holy kiss." Paul's words remind us that appropriate physical affection was to be an expression of loving care among believers. How much more should married couples freely share physical closeness and affectionate language.

Teresa and I were reminded of the power of affection in a relationship after spending several hours with Billy and Kay, whose marriage was in trouble. We worked through several issues with the couple, including confession and forgiveness of the ways they had hurt each other over the years.

Two weeks later, we saw them again and asked, "What are the most positive things that have happened in your relationship since we last met?" Kay told of Billy's increased sensitivity to some of her needs and his initiative in setting up a special date for them, including arranging the baby-sitting. It was a very positive report.

Then we turned to Billy. "When we left you two weeks ago," he began, "we felt very close to each other because some significant healing had begun in our relationship. A lot of good things have happened since then, but the best thing for me happened as we were driving away from here two weeks ago." Tears came to Billy's eyes as he continued. "Kay slid over next to me in the car, put her arm around my shoulder, and gave me a gentle squeeze. And it meant so much to me."

Many wonderful things had taken place, but at the top of his list was a momentary, warm embrace, which had happened two weeks earlier. That's a glimpse of the power of affection!

**What might the need for affection sound like?** "When you hold me close and speak to me tenderly, I feel loved. Your gentle touch, warm embrace, and loving words help me stay emotionally connected to you. I don't ever want your sweet words and affectionate actions to become routine."

**What might affection sound like?** "You are so precious to me"; "You mean the world to me. I don't know what I would do without you"; "I was just thinking about how special you are to me and how much I love you"; "I'm so happy to be with you"; "I feel so close to you."

**What might affection look like?** In a marriage relationship, embraces, private winks, loving smiles, hand-holding, kisses, and body rubs have great need-meeting value, even when they do not lead to sex—maybe particularly when they do not lead to sex. Affection may look like a quiet, romantic walk, sitting close on a park bench while feeding squirrels, listening to love songs together in a dimly lit room, or staying close in a large group.

### 8. Respect: Valuing and Esteeming Your Partner

Teresa has a wonderful way of ministering to my need for respect. I have a lot of grand ideas about our ministry, marriage, and family life, and some of them are pretty wild. Whenever I toss out a new idea, she may think it's crazy or that it will never work—and sometimes she's right on both counts. She could easily make me feel like a clay pigeon in a skeet shoot—quickly shooting down any ideas I toss out. But as God has continued to teach us about his plan for intimacy, she always hears me out without passing judgment because she realizes my need of the moment is for her to respect me and my ideas. Only later, perhaps at bedtime, will she take my hand tenderly and say something like, "I have been thinking about what you said earlier, and I'm beginning to wonder if..." And she shares her concern and becomes a vehicle of God's counsel. Even if I abandon my "grand idea," I still feel valued and respected.

*WE were created with the capacity and need to receive love and care through affectionate touch and loving words.*

We all need people to value us, to recognize our worth, and to esteem us. You communicate esteem when you respect your spouse's ideas, opinions, wishes, personal space, and schedule, and when you seek his or her perspective on an issue or decision. *W*E all need people to value us, to recognize our worth, and to esteem us. You convey worth when you affirm his or her strengths and gifts. When you respect your spouse, you are experiencing 1 Peter 2:17: "Show respect for everyone. Love your Christian brothers and sisters. Fear God. Show respect for the king" (NLT). And respect shown to your spouse is respect shown to Christ.

**What might the need for respect sound like?** "It means so much to me when you ask for my advice or opinion, when you involve me when making plans for us, and when you talk to me before making changes that affect me or my schedule."

**What might respect sound like?** "You're so good at helping me think through these details"; "I need your input on this because your insights are so valuable to me"; "May I share what I'm dealing with so you can tell me what you think?"; "What do you think we should do?"; "We may have to change plans, but I want to talk it through with you first."

**What might respect look like?** Respect may be demonstrated through being punctual with your spouse, respecting his or her schedule; allowing your spouse time alone, respecting his or her need for personal space; staying within the family budget, respecting your spouse's sense of financial security; caring for your spouse's personal property; valuing your spouse's ideas.

### 9. Security: Protecting Your Partner from Harm, Fear, and Loss

It had always puzzled me that Teresa seemed almost paranoid about locking up the house at night. Locks and dead bolts are not something I usually think about. But before we headed off to bed,

Teresa would methodically make the rounds, checking every door and window to assure that we were sealed in for the night. And there were other situations in which her high personal need to be safe and protected was evident. As I came to know Teresa more deeply, I discerned that her "need of the moment" in those times was for security. I realized that if I was going to minister to Teresa's need for security, I had to establish new patterns of behavior.

As a result, I committed myself to be more security conscious, because in her world, security was a high priority. Today, activities such as locking up at night and parking in well-lit areas are important to me because they are important to Teresa. This is what security looks like to Teresa, so this is one clearly defined way I can meet one of her intimacy needs. And when God empowers me to meet her need, a measure of her aloneness is removed and intimacy results.

Security defines our need for protection from danger, deprivation, and harmful relationships. We all need to experience freedom from fears and to feel safe from physical, emotional, relational, and financial peril. We need to sense that we will be provided for and cared for. When we provide security for our partners, we are experiencing Psalm 122:6-8: "May those who love you be secure. May there be peace within your walls and security within your citadels. . . . I will say, 'Peace be within you' " (NIV).

We feel satisfied when our current needs are being met, but we feel secure when we are confident our future needs will also be met. For example, your spouse may be satisfied with a comfortable home and nice clothes. But he or she will feel secure in your ongoing commitment to provide for physical and material needs in the future, to maintain a growing relationship, and to pursue spiritual growth.

**What might the need for security sound like?** "I want to feel assured that everything between us is all right, that you are committed for the long haul as we grow through our differences. I want to feel safe in our financial dealings, investments, and retirement

95

planning. I want to feel safe from harmful social relationships and physical danger."

**What might security sound like?** "I love you now, and I will always love you, no matter what happens"; "If I could do it all over again, you are the one I would choose to spend my life with"; "I am committed to you, and as God allows and provides, I will meet your needs both now and in the future."

**What might security look like?** Physical security might appear as joint ownership of all property and possessions; an updated will; promptly paid bills; a savings plan; paid-up health, life, and disability insurance; a home-security system; careful driving; or an adequate retirement plan. Relational and emotional security may be visible as having a group of trusted mutual friends, spending time together nurturing your own relationship, setting goals for the future and working on them together, or making plans for children.

### 10. Approval: Affirming Your Partner

We all need to sense that others think favorably of us, and we all need affirmation as persons. A poignant example of approval is at the baptism of Jesus, when the Father spoke from heaven for all around to hear, "You are my Son, whom I love; with you I am well pleased" (Mark 1:11, NIV). When you seek to meet your spouse's need for approval, you are experiencing Romans 14:18: "If you serve Christ with this attitude, you will please God. And other people will approve of you, too" (NLT).

Meeting the need for approval should focus more on your spouse's intrinsic worth as God's creation than on what he or she has accomplished. Approval does not highlight what has been accomplished as much as why it was accomplished. Showing approval places value on your spouse's character qualities and gifts that enable success—qualities such as determination, persistence, creativity, reliability, or attention to detail. Demonstrating love through approval requires that you really know your spouse. As you seek to discern his or her attributes, gifts, and qualities, you will better know how to minister approval according to the need of the moment.

**What might the need for approval sound like?** "I need you to appreciate me for everything I do, but I need just as much for you to approve of me for why I do what I do. It is important to me that you see beyond my deeds to affirm my abilities and motivations."

**What might approval sound like?** "The dinner with our friends was perfect. Your ability to create such a warm and inviting atmosphere around the table is amazing. Your gift of hospitality really shines through"; "You are so thorough and disciplined about checking the bank statements. I'm so proud of you"; "The garden looks great. I admire your creativity and attention to detail in caring for the yard."

**What might approval look like?** Approval may look a lot like appreciation: a warm smile, an affirming hug, a card, note, or gift. But the emphasis of your approval will be on character qualities and gifts rather than on specific deeds or accomplishments.

*MEETING the need for approval should focus more on your spouse's intrinsic worth as God's creation than on what he or she has accomplished.*

THE IMPORTANCE OF MEETING THE NEED OF THE MOMENT

God designed that a couple's biblically valid intimacy needs be met in significant ways through relationship with one another. As a husband and wife are with each other and meeting needs through the highs and lows of daily life, they help to remove each other's aloneness and to deepen their intimacy. But when we fail to become caringly involved with our spouse by ignoring or overlooking intimacy needs, the result may be a complex and painful chain reaction that is not good. For example:

- A spouse who is not comforted in emotional pain may not find healing.
- A spouse who is not granted sufficient attention may not feel valued by God and others.
- A spouse who does not receive acceptance may have difficulty grasping his or her worth in God's eyes.
- A spouse who is not properly appreciated may struggle with feelings of insignificance.
- A spouse who does not receive support may feel overwhelmed and hopeless.
- A spouse who is not encouraged may grow weary and give up.
- A spouse who does not receive sufficient affection may struggle with receiving love and feel unlovable.
- A spouse who does not receive respect may feel ignored and unimportant.
- A spouse who does not sense security in the relationship may be paralyzed by fear and distrust.
- A spouse who does not receive approval may not feel valued as a person.

A sense of insignificance, hopelessness, unhealed emotional pain, fear, or distrust is a telltale sign of aloneness—the tragic result of unmet needs. The good news is that Christ stands ready to involve you in removing your spouse's aloneness by meeting these intimacy needs. God is our need-meeting source, and he desires to empower you to express your love to your spouse in need-meeting ways. Tapping into the power to meet needs is the focus of the next chapter.

CHAPTER 6

# The Power of a Three-Dimensional Marriage

William and Linda were in their middle thirties and had been married for ten years. They met with Teresa and me during one of our conferences, and when they sat down, their body language spoke volumes. They put as much space between themselves as they could arrange.

Linda got right to the point. She said to us, "I've heard that you can fix stale relationships, and ours is pretty stale." She went on to elaborate how their marriage had become routine, adding that William had lost motivation to work on the relationship. She explained that she felt robbed of the intimacy they both were due.

When she finished, I looked over at William and asked, "How would you characterize your relationship with Linda?"

He nodded and said, "Yes, there is a distance between us. I agree that our love for each other has become stale. And to be honest with you, I have lost a lot of motivation to get us back on track. I guess I need to know what to do in our relationship to regain that motivation."

William and Linda had bought into the common misconception that a successful, loving marriage is primarily the result of the horizontal relationship between husband and wife. They knew that they should love each other and remain committed to each other. But when the love between them cooled, they figured it was up to them to find some way to fire up their motivation and passion.

Linda particularly seemed to be looking to Teresa and me for some new tip to fix William or some poignant exhortation to awaken his love for her.

*M*ARRIAGE *is a three-dimensional relationship: spouses relating to one another, and each spouse relating to God.*

If marriage were solely a horizontal relationship between the two human participants, Linda would be right: All they would needed to ignite their love was a good pep talk and a few dynamic exercises on clearer communication, better sex, or any number of marital-intimacy skills. But marriage is not just a horizontal relationship between husband and wife; it is also a vertical relationship between God and both partners. In reality, marriage is a three-dimensional relationship: spouses relating to one another, and each spouse relating to God.

## ROBBING GOD IN MARRIAGE

William and Linda needed to go beyond "fixing" their marriage on the horizontal level and tap into the ultimate power source for their love. That power source is a vertical relationship with God based on the Great Commandment of Christ: "'You shall love the Lord your God with all your heart, and with all your soul, and with all your mind.' This is the great and foremost commandment. And a second is like it, 'You shall love your neighbor as yourself'" (Matt. 22:37-39). We shared with Linda and William that their love for one another could be revitalized and sustained only as it was expressed through their love for God. When God is left out of the experience, love grows cold.

Then we said, "It could be that your love for each other has grown stale because God is loving your spouse, but he is doing so alone. Consequently, you are robbing each other of love and intimacy, and you are robbing God of the joy he seeks from your marriage."

William was troubled by this thought. "I'm not robbing God of anything," he insisted. "I may have caused Linda some heartache, but I'm not depriving God of anything."

But he *was* depriving God. Scripture makes it clear that our relationships with others have a direct bearing on our relationship with God. In Malachi 3:8, God confronted the children of Israel: "Will a man rob God? Yet you are robbing Me!" The people were withholding their tithes and offerings, which were used to sustain the Levites, who ministered in the temple. Yet God regarded the action as a direct assault on him. In God's view, robbing the Levites was the same as robbing him.

God intended William and Linda to receive an important measure of his love through one another. When they did not receive the love they needed, they felt deprived—and so did God. The same is true in your marriage. You have been called by God to love your spouse by knowing that person intimately, being with him or her emotionally through all of life's experiences, and meeting valid intimacy needs. When you fail to demonstrate your love in these ways, your spouse will feel deprived. And God also feels deprived because you are withholding your love from him as much as from your spouse.

You may find it difficult to comprehend that an infinite God longs to receive your love through your spouse and that he feels personally deprived when you fail to love your spouse. But the account of Jesus' encounter with ten lepers, recorded in Luke 17:12-19, further underscores how our actions in relationships affect God.

Here were ten men—their flesh rotting, extremities gone. Outcasts of society, they were forced to identify their contagious condition by crying, "Unclean, unclean." Isolated from loved ones, they were united by a common misery: leprosy.

*SCRIPTURE makes it clear that our relationships with others have a direct bearing on our relationship with God.*

Then word spread through the leper colony about a young Jewish man named Jesus, who with tenderness and compassion healed those who called on his name. So in their desperation, these ten lepers found him. But instead of crying, "Unclean, unclean," they cried, "Jesus, Master, have mercy on us!" (v. 13).

Jesus responded, " 'Go and show yourselves to the priests.' And it came about that as they were going, they were cleansed" (v. 14).

As the ten saw the disease vanish before their eyes, multiple emotions must have flooded their hearts: bewilderment, ecstasy, hope. But one man was overcome by overwhelming gratitude. He reversed direction immediately, glorifying God with a loud voice, and made his way back to Jesus. Falling at Jesus' feet, this one cleansed leper gave thanks to the One who had made him whole. The priests were always on call at the synagogue, and there was ample time to be formally declared pure. But at this moment the man's heart was fixed on one thing: expressing gratitude to Jesus. And, irony of ironies, this man was a despised Samaritan, not a Jew.

Jesus could have said something like, "You're welcome. It was nice of you to come back and thank me." Or he might have said, "Don't mention it, I'm just doing my job." But instead, he said, "Were there not ten cleansed? But the nine—where are they? Was no one found who turned back to give glory to God, except this foreigner?" (verses 17-18). Could this response possibly reflect Jesus' disappointment or hurt that only one person came back to thank him? Might he have been waiting to rejoice with all ten men, only to be deprived of that joy by the nine who never returned?

How many marriages have left Jesus feeling disappointed and hurt? Couples exchange wedding vows at the church and then speed off to the honeymoon, leaving Christ standing at the altar— alone. Has he been left out of your marriage, loving your spouse without you and deprived of the joy of receiving your love and gratitude as you minister to your spouse?

As your colleague, Christ desires to help you know and love your spouse as only he can—and he receives great joy from that. But he also yearns to be your companion in marriage, entering into the joy of your love as you meet your spouse's intimacy needs. Yes, he is committed to minister to your spouse whether or not you join him. But he does not want to do it alone! Could Christ be hurting over being deprived of the pleasure of joining you in loving your spouse? Could it be that the God who is love is disappointed when he misses out on the joy of your intimacy as a couple?

*As your colleague, Christ desires to help you know and love your spouse as only he can—and he receives great joy from that.*

When I surprised Teresa with Sweet'n Low on our trip, it was my colleague in marriage who prompted me to bring the packets. I am convinced I never would have thought of it without him. But when I handed Teresa a pink packet and that endearing smile flooded her face, I sensed more than God's pleasure that Teresa's need for attention was being met. It was as if I heard my companion whispering in my ear, "You did well, Son! You made your sweetheart so happy when you expressed such loving attention, and in doing so you ministered attention to me too!"

### How Your Love for Your Spouse Ministers to Christ

We know that Christ is worthy to receive "power and riches and wisdom and might and honor and glory and blessing" (Rev. 5:12). But what kind of blessing does Christ receive out of your marriage when you meet your spouse's needs?

Jesus said of the ministry we share with others, "I assure you, when you did it to one of the least of these my brothers and sisters, you were doing it to me!" (Matt. 25:40, NLT). In this wonderful, mysterious union of husband, wife, and Christ, Christ is a corecipient of your ministry to your spouse. When you comfort your partner, Christ receives comfort. When you provide needed attention to your partner, Christ receives attention. Every time God empowers you to bless your spouse by meeting intimacy needs, Christ is also blessed by that ministry.

*E*VERY time God empowers you to bless your spouse by meeting intimacy needs, Christ is also blessed by that ministry.

Earlier, we related the story of Teresa as a five-year-old climbing a ladder to the top of the house in search of her daddy's attention. The night she told that story is when I sensed Christ's call to be yoked with him as a colleague in meeting Teresa's intimacy needs. As I embraced Teresa and wept for her, I sensed that God was also weeping for her. My wife experienced the blessing of being comforted and cared for, and I was blessed as God shared a portion of his loving comfort through me.

But more than this happened on that night. Not only did Teresa and I give and receive the blessing of comfort, but Christ also received the comfort I was ministering to my wife. I realized then that I had not only robbed Teresa of the attention she needed, but I had also robbed God of attention. In a mysterious way, the Savior had actually suffered due to my neglect of Teresa. She had been wanting for attention, and I had not provided it. I sensed Christ saying, "I assure you, when you refused to help the least of these my brothers and sisters, you were refusing to help me" (Matt. 25:45, NLT).

That night I not only embraced and wept for a wonderful wife, but I embraced and wept for a wounded Savior. The God of all comfort involved me in ministering his comfort to both Teresa and Christ, whom I had wounded. Christ is worthy to be blessed by our marriage in very specific ways. He is worthy of receiving comfort, and he did in fact receive comfort as I comforted Teresa. He is worthy of receiving attention, and he did in fact receive attention as I began to become more caringly involved in Teresa's life.

God is worthy to receive something very specific out of your marriage relationship as well. Through the mysterious union of Christ and his church, Christ has experienced your affliction and joy. When you rejoice or weep with your spouse, when you meet his or her intimacy needs, your companion in loving that dear one receives very specific loving ministry as well. But when you ignore your spouse's needs, Christ also experiences the neglect.

In his description of Christ's body, Paul wrote, "If one member suffers, all the members suffer with it; if one member is honored, all the members rejoice with it" (1 Cor. 12:26). Christ, as the head of that body, also suffers and rejoices as the members of his body suffer and rejoice. Your loving ministry—or lack of it—to your partner has a direct impact on your Savior.

## THE MOTIVATION FOR COMPASSION

The real power and true motivation behind caring love are found in our vertical relationship with God. The apostle Paul spoke of this passion in Philippians 3:8-10. "I count all things to be loss in view of the surpassing value of knowing Christ Jesus my Lord . . . that I may know Him, and the power of His resurrection and the fellowship of His sufferings."

This truth gripped me several years ago in a surprising and dramatic way. I had preached on Philippians 3:8-10 one Sunday morning in a church away from home. The theme of my sermon that day was knowing Christ and the power of his resurrection and the fellowship of his sufferings. I had always assumed this passage referred to the crosses we must bear for being Christians. But after all that God began to show me that day, I realized that I had no idea what it meant.

*THE real power and true motivation behind caring love are found in our vertical relationship with God.*

In my message that Sunday, I had also read a number of passages describing Christ's suffering, from the Last Supper to Gethsemane to Calvary. Driving the rental car back to the airport after the service, I began to think about those passages and the rejection, humiliation, and pain Jesus suffered. Unexpected tears began to fill my eyes. Soon I was weeping so profusely that I could no longer drive safely. I had to pull to the side of the road and stop the car. I wept openly, without explanation, for several minutes.

As I wept, I tried to figure out what the emotional outburst was all about. I asked myself, *Why are you crying?* The answer came almost as quickly. *I think I'm crying for Jesus. I think I'm feeling sad for the pain he must have felt. Maybe I'm entering into fellowship with his suffering.*

I had never cried for Jesus before. I had never participated in his suffering as I did that day. I had studied the topic. I had exegeted the passages and preached on them. But that day beside the highway, it was as if God said, "David, you know a lot about my Son's suffering. I would like to help you experience these verses in order to deepen your love for me and Teresa and others."

From that point on, I began to know Christ and experience the fellowship of his sufferings in a brand-new way. That roadside encounter dramatically changed my life and ministry. It unlocked to my understanding the motivation behind loving my wife and family.

We believe that the power and motivation to know your spouse and lovingly meet his or her needs is found in an intimate love relationship with Christ. Jesus told his disciples, "If you love Me, you will keep My commandments" (John 14:15). Motivation for obedience and the power to minister to your partner are rooted in your love relationship with God. And as you walk in daily intimacy with Christ, his constraining love will fill and empower you for obedient, loving ministry.

Being with Christ is how you capture his heart and love as he loves. As you sorrow over the things that bring sorrow to God's heart, you are prepared to be with your spouse in his or her sorrow. As you come to care more deeply for Jesus, the Man of Sorrows, your care for your spouse will deepen. Your motivation to lovingly meet the needs of your dear one will dramatically increase as you realize that when you minister to your spouse, you minister to Christ.

## MINISTERING TO THE SAVIOR: A MEDITATION

Until we come to care deeply and intimately for the Man of Sorrows, who suffered for us, we have little hope of sustaining a deepened caring involvement with our spouses, our families, or others. And a significant way we can be with Jesus and care more deeply for him is to enter into the fellowship of his sufferings.

The only way I know to share with you what I mean is to walk with you through a simple exercise of experiencing several Bible passages, beginning with Philippians 3:10, "I want to know Christ . . . and the fellowship of sharing in his sufferings" (NIV).

If you are taking notes or highlighting passages as you read this book, you might find it more helpful to put down your pen for a few minutes. If you are a speed-reader, I suggest that you slow to a contemplative pace for the rest of this chapter. The purpose of the next several paragraphs is not to get more Bible facts into your head. Rather, this brief Scripture meditation is offered to allow your heart to connect with God's heart. As you encounter Christ and his suffering and begin to care for him more deeply, you will be better prepared to express your love more deeply to your spouse.

Come with us into the New Testament for an intimate picture of God's heart. Jesus Christ was not only fully God but also fully man. In his humanity he had the normal human needs for air, food, water, and sleep to sustain him physically. He also needed things such as comfort, encouragement, support, appreciation, and affection, just as we do. He even hurt the way we hurt, yet he did not sin. No wonder Isaiah described him as "a man of sorrows, acquainted with bitterest grief. . . . He was despised, and we did not care" (Isa. 53:3, NLT).

When Jesus called his disciples to be with him, they had opportunities to rejoice with him in his times of joy and comfort him in his disappointments. But did Jesus find that kind of companionship in these twelve men?

Luke 9 recounts how Jesus took Peter, James, and John to the mountain to pray. But the disciples fell asleep. While Jesus was praying, "the appearance of His face became different, and His clothing became white and gleaming. And behold, two men were talking with Him; and they were Moses and Elijah" (verses 29-30). The disciples awoke to the astonishing scene. As Moses and Elijah departed, Peter said to Jesus, "'Master, it is good for us to be here; and let us make three tabernacles: one for You, and one for Moses, and one for Elijah'—not realizing what he was saying" (v. 33).

But instead of the disciples' rejoicing with Christ in his moment of glory, Peter wanted to establish a headquarters for the Messiah and the two patriarchs. Instead of proclaiming Christ worthy to receive honor, and joining in the praise with Moses and Elijah, his followers wanted to institutionalize the moment.

While Peter was speaking, a voice came from a cloud saying, "'This is My Son, My chosen one; listen to Him!' And when the voice had spoken, Jesus was found alone" (Luke 9:35-37). What impact do you think the disciples' response had on Jesus in that glorious moment? He could have desired that his dearest friends rejoice with him, but instead they analyzed the event and wanted to build a monument to it. It was a time of unsurpassed joy for the Master, but on a human level, he rejoiced alone. Can you sense his disappointment?

Now let's follow Jesus to the Upper Room, only hours before the atrocities of the trial, the merciless beatings, and the crucifixion.

Cloistered with the twelve men into whom he had poured his life, he breaks bread and says, "Take, eat; this is My body" (Matt. 26:26). Then he lifts the cup and says, "Drink from it, all of you; for this is My blood" (verses 27-28). Consider his vulnerability, his openness to speak of his death. He has never before shared with such shocking clarity.

But how do the disciples respond to Jesus' openness and transparency? When we look at Luke's account of this occasion, we learn that the disciples seem unaffected by the suffering their Lord has just shared. In fact, "they began to argue among themselves as to who would be the greatest in the coming Kingdom" (Luke 22:24, NLT). Did such indifference and self-centeredness hurt the Savior? He agonizes that his body will soon be broken and his blood shed, while the men he counted as friends argue over their own status. Can you hurt with him at such insensitivity? Can you find fellowship with his suffering?

After Judas leaves to betray him, Christ speaks to the remaining eleven. He continues to minister out of selfless concern for his friends: "Do not let your hearts be troubled. Trust in God; trust also in me" (John 14:1, NIV). Jesus lovingly speaks of preparing a place for his disciples and returning to take them home. It is this unwavering concern for the disciples, even to the very end, that makes their insensitivity and selfishness so painfully cruel. He concludes, "I am the way and the truth and the life. No one comes to the Father except through me" (v. 6, NIV).

But Philip's response must have slashed through the Savior's heart: "Lord, show us the Father and that will be enough for us" (v. 8, NIV).

> *JESUS lovingly speaks of preparing a place for his disciples and returning to take them home. It is this unwavering concern for the disciples, even to the very end, that makes their insensitivity and selfishness so painfully cruel.*

After more than three years of day-to-day contact with God in human flesh, Philip only wants to see the Father. What rejection! Can you hear the pain in Jesus' reply? He asked, "Don't you know me, Philip, even after I have been among you such a long time?" (v. 9, NIV).

Allow yourself to experience the sorrow and pain Jesus suffered. The powerful impact of this verse brought tears to my eyes that day beside the road. It was as if the suffering Savior spoke the same words to my heart: "David, have you been with me this long and don't really know me?" Is your heart stirred to sadness for a hurting Savior?

Now let us follow our Lord and the eleven into the Garden of Gethsemane. Picture yourself walking among the trees with the disciples, following the Master we love. His steps appear agonizingly slow and deliberate as the weight of his impending death descends on him. His breath comes in short, labored gasps. The mounting stress bows his back and forces from him a low moan, then another, as if the heavy wooden cross were already on his shoulder. Meanwhile, we notice the disciples around us are puzzled at his behavior, perhaps thinking him suddenly ill.

Reaching our destination, the Master turns to us. His countenance appears clouded with gloom. Perspiration streams from his brow and drips from his hair and beard. "I must . . . I must go . . . just a little farther." He looks past us to Peter, James, and John, his closest and dearest friends on earth. Imagine his imploring words, "Come with me, my friends. I need you now. I really need you."

Leaving the others behind, Jesus and his three closest disciples continue trudging up the darkened garden hillside. We follow them. The Master's body appears to convulse from the mounting grief. His low moans turn to sustained cries of the deepest pain. Jesus can hardly get his next words out. His voice seems strained with emotion. "My soul is overwhelmed with sorrow to the point of death. Stay here and keep watch with me" (Matt. 26:38, NIV).

He leaves us behind and staggers farther up the knoll, bracing himself on tree stumps and boulders. Loud cries of travail roll from him. Then he writhes and sobs and prays.

At a distance from the Savior, we huddle with Peter, James, and John to watch. Soon the three fall asleep.

The Son of God faces the darkest hour in the history of creation. The One who knew no sin would soon become sin for his disciples—for you and me. He has vulnerably sought the prayerful support of Peter, James, and John. These men love the Master dearly. They have left their careers to follow him. They have walked with him, sat at his feet, and leaned on his breast. But now they seem oblivious to the Master's need. On the human level, Jesus is hurting, and he is alone.

He returns to the place where we are watching the heartrending drama. Imagine as he looks down at his dearest friends, who are asleep. Tears, soil, and blood streak his face and stain his cloak. He moves past us and wakes the men. Let yourself sense the pain-filled loneliness and grief of the Savior's heart as he asks, "Could you men not keep watch with me for one hour?" (Matt. 26:40, NIV).

See the pain of disappointment in his eyes as he returns to his place of agonizing prayer.

Amazingly, the scene plays out again and then again. Three times the Master shares his pain and need with his closest friends, and three times they let him down. Do you care for him in his pain? Can you hurt with him? Can you fellowship with his suffering?

Now Judas and the soldiers appear on the scene. We are close enough to see Jesus betrayed with a sign of affection from Judas. Do you feel the sting in that kiss? A scuffle breaks out with the soldiers, and the disciples flee into the night to save their own lives. How does it affect Jesus to be abandoned by those he loves?

Peter follows in the shadows at a safe distance. But then he is discovered in the temple courtyard and accused of being one of

Christ's disciples. He curses and swears vehemently, "I don't know this man" (Mark 14:71, NIV).

Jesus looks directly at him. The pain in his gaze is no longer that of abandonment but of betrayal. Can you hurt for this One who is both despised and rejected as Peter disavows their friendship? Can you hurt for him?

Allow yourself to fellowship with the suffering of Jesus. Sorrow for him. Grieve his loss, his abandonment, his betrayal. He was discouraged, and no one encouraged him. He was rejected, and no one accepted him. He was forsaken, and no one supported him. Can you feel his grief? Are you moved with compassion for a Savior who suffered such aloneness?

Now contemplate for a moment this God-man who is not confined to human time. Our history past is his eternal present. His rejection and aloneness are as real to him today as they were two thousand years ago. No person encouraged the Savior or accepted him or comforted him or supported him. But someone is here in the twenty-first century to do just that. And to the extent you comfort and accept and support and encourage your spouse and others, you do it to him!

Who is getting the most out of your marriage? Consider the depths of pain and sorrow that the God-man endured to save a lost world. It defies comprehension, doesn't it? Now contemplate how your loving care to your wife or husband ministers a measure of that same care to the Man of Sorrows. It is beyond understanding, but I believe that when we meet the intimacy needs of our spouses, Christ gets even more out of our relationship than we do!

More important, what does it do to your heart to know that you are actually ministering to Christ when you meet your spouse's needs? Does it not engender such a deep and pure motivation to love Christ and your spouse? Is that not the compelling, arresting, constraining love of Christ at work in your life?

Pause right now to tell God how humbled and grateful you

are that he wants to receive ministry from you through your spouse. Declare to him that he is worthy to receive glory, power, and blessing. Declare that you, as part of his creation, want to bring him the pleasure he deserves. Tell him you want to minister to him loving comfort, attention, acceptance, appreciation, support, encouragement, affection, respect, security, and approval through loving your spouse in this manner. Express to him your awe that he is such an intimate part of your marriage. Worship him as the only One worthy to receive glory, honor, and praise.

*I believe that when we meet the intimacy needs of our spouses, Christ gets even more out of our relationship than we do!*

PART
three

God's Conduit

*Our Hurts Are Healed*

# CHAPTER 7

# Nurturing Intimacy in a Pain-Filled World

Sarah heard the back door open and glanced at her watch. Eddie was an hour and a half late for supper. He had promised to be on time, and he hadn't called to let her know he would be late. "Sorry, honey, but the meeting ran later than I expected," Eddie explained matter-of-factly as he set down his briefcase. Sarah said nothing as she placed supper on the table and sat down.

"Smells good," Eddie said, joining her at the table. "What do you call this dish?" Sarah remained silent, and soon Eddie heard the silence loudly and clearly. "Darling, I said I was sorry, but I just couldn't help it," he lamented in his own defense.

Sarah finally broke her silence. "You couldn't help it? What stopped you from picking up the phone and simply letting me know you were going to be late?"

"Well, I didn't think . . ."

"That's the problem," Sarah interrupted. "You didn't think about me—that I've been sitting here for an hour and a half not knowing what was wrong. That is so inconsiderate!"

Sarah pushed back her chair and stood up, tears filling her eyes. "It just hurts that you don't care enough to call." Then she stormed out of the kitchen, and Eddie got the silent treatment for the next two days.

Even if you and your spouse have not clashed over this same issue, you have experienced similar conflicts in countless other areas. Pain is inevitable in a marriage relationship, whether it is caused intentionally or unintentionally. You can and should take steps to reduce the emotional pain you cause your spouse. But as long as you are human and imperfect, you cannot completely avoid causing hurt, and neither can your spouse.

Even if you *could* stop hurting each other completely, there are other sources of pain in your lives you cannot control. You and your spouse can be emotionally hurt by inconsiderate colleagues at work, neighbors, friends, parents, other relatives, or complete strangers. Rarely does a day go by that someone doesn't inflict emotional pain on each of you through words, actions, or the neglectful omission of one or both.

In addition to unavoidable day-to-day pain, you and your spouse may carry some lingering pain from sad childhood experiences. Or you may have issues of imagined pain, such as a perceived rejection that was never intended. But imagined pain still hurts, and like all other emotional pain, it must be resolved. Intimacy in marriage is encouraged when husbands and wives become conduits for God's glory as he provides healing through us for life's inevitable hurts.

This brings us to a third response to the vital question "What does God want out of your marriage?" First, God is seeking a *colleague* in the ministry of loving your spouse. When you and your spouse become God's colleagues, yoked together with him to love each other, your longing to deeply know and be known by each other can be fulfilled.

Second, God is seeking a *companion* in your marriage, someone who, through meeting your spouse's intimacy needs in the marriage relationship, will also minister to him. When you and your spouse become his companions, your longing to be cherished and to have your deepest needs met can be fulfilled.

Third, God is seeking a *conduit* for his presence in your marriage. He longs to exhibit through you and your marriage his giving heart, his unconditional love, and his faithfulness. Also, in a pain-filled world, he desires to be your Great Physician, who provides the healing you need. When you and your spouse become his conduits, he receives the glory he deserves in your marriage, and your longings for healing from emotional pain can be fulfilled.

In order to become a conduit of God's healing and glory in your marriage, you must understand how to respond to emotional pain in each other. Unhealed inner pain, regardless of its origin, is a major obstacle to intimacy in a relationship. Even the pain you and your spouse experienced before meeting each other can hinder you from deepening your relationship together. If God is to receive abundant glory through your marriage, if you and your spouse are to be healed, and if the intimacy of your relationship is to grow ever deeper, you must learn to deal with hurts in God's way.

## THE PAIN OF UNMET NEEDS

Virtually every emotional wound is the result of an intimacy need going unmet. God has created us with basic relational needs, and he is the ultimate source for meeting those needs. Yet he also calls us into partnership with him to meet the needs of those around us. When we fail to express God's love in practical, need-meeting ways, those needs go unmet, and pain is the result.

The diagram of the cup (see page 121) is a picture of how our emotional capacity can become so full of painful emotions that overflowing symptoms cause additional pain for us and others. A quick glance into Sarah's past illustrates how Eddie's insensitivity about calling home when he would be late touched a deep pain from her past, causing her cup to overflow.

"I don't see how we will have the time or

*$\mathcal{P}$AIN is inevitable in a marriage relationship, whether it is caused intentionally or unintentionally.*

119

money for the vacation this year, Marsha," Henry said to his wife over supper.

"But the children are looking forward to a vacation, honey," Marsha replied, "and you need a break from work. Can't you make the time?"

"I think you can do it, Daddy," injected ten-year-old Sarah enthusiastically. "You can take the time for a vacation."

"Well, what you think doesn't count here, Sarah," scolded her father. Sarah dropped her head, feeling stung by her father's rejection.

Little Sarah grew up being told that her opinion was not important to her father. As a result, her need for respect went largely unmet. So when Sarah married Eddie, she brought into their relationship a high need for others to value her time, her thoughts, and her efforts. Whenever Eddie fails to call her about being late, it not only disappoints and hurts Sarah but also triggers an unhealed childhood hurt that Eddie had nothing to do with. Of course, his own inconsiderate and disrespectful behavior simply adds to Sarah's pain.

When intimacy needs in your spouse go unmet, emotional pain is experienced. It may be a small wound, and you may not even be aware of the pain your partner has experienced, but the pain is real. And if your spouse is already hurting in that area, the wound may be compounded by negative memories and past experiences. If that pain is not addressed in a loving, biblical manner, the following painful chain reaction may result (see diagram on page 122):

1. **An intimacy need goes unmet.** It may be the result of neglect, abuse, criticism, rejection, or careless words or actions. Eddie was inconsiderate of Sarah's time and effort, failing to value her and respect her needs and hopes.

2. **An unmet need often prompts faulty thinking.** When Eddie failed to arrive on time or call, Sarah's thoughts may have gone something like this: *Eddie is being very inconsiderate. He just doesn't care about me. Maybe what I think and want is unimportant, just like*

# The Symptoms
# of a Full Cup

Escape into… Work, Drugs,
Infidelity, Pornography, etc.

Impatience, Quick Temper

Depressed Mood

Loss of Energy,
Concentration

Physical Side Effects

Physical:
Sleep/Appetite
Disturbances

Loss of Positive
Emotions like Joy, Love,
Affection, Romance

**Biblical Antidotes:**

Romans 8:1

Condemnation

1 John 1:9
James 5:16

Guilt

**Build-up
of
Painful
Emotions**

1 John 4:18
2 Timothy 1:7
1 Peter 5:7

Fear, Anxiety, Insecurities

Ephesians 4:31-32
Proverbs 15:1

Anger, Resentment

Romans 12:15b
Matthew 5:4

Hurt, Sadness,
Disappointment

# Emotional Capacity

*Daddy said.* This is unhealthy thinking. Eddie *does* care about Sarah, but his failure to meet her need for respect has prompted this inaccurate generalization.

**3. Faulty thinking often leads to painful, unhealed feelings.** Sarah was hurt by Eddie's failure and the thoughts it prompted. She felt unimportant and unloved. And by storming out of the room and giving Eddie the silent treatment, her bad feelings went unhealed and, in fact, were compounded by her wrong response.

**4. Painful feelings are often expressed in unproductive behaviors.** Sarah's forty-eight-hour cold shoulder could be considered a manipulative game or a punishing retaliation, both of which are unhealthy and unproductive to an intimate relationship.

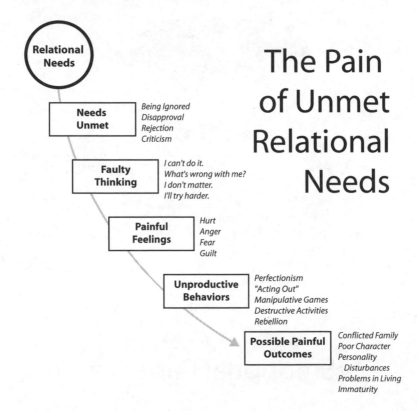

**The Pain of Unmet Relational Needs**

**Relational Needs**

**Needs Unmet**
Being Ignored
Disapproval
Rejection
Criticism

**Faulty Thinking**
I can't do it.
What's wrong with me?
I don't matter.
I'll try harder.

**Painful Feelings**
Hurt
Anger
Fear
Guilt

**Unproductive Behaviors**
Perfectionism
"Acting Out"
Manipulative Games
Destructive Activities
Rebellion

**Possible Painful Outcomes**
Conflicted Family
Poor Character
Personality
  Disturbances
Problems in Living
Immaturity

**5. Unproductive behaviors produce painful outcomes.** Sarah's sense of personal value and worth was undermined. If this pain is not healed, she may establish a pattern of anger or cycles of withdrawal that will rob her and Eddie of the intimacy they desire in their relationship. The diagram illustrates the potential pain of not meeting relational needs.

## HURL, HIDE, OR HEAL

What happens when someone gets trapped in the painful and damaging chain reaction of unmet needs, unhealthy thinking, unhealed emotions, and unproductive behaviors? Andy is a graphic example of painful outcomes, but he is also an example of hope in the healing of deep emotional pain.

Andy was big, burly, and mean, kind of like an NFL linebacker—except Andy didn't play football. He was just a very big, very angry forty-year-old man. Although he had recently become a Christian, Andy had a history of violence that often got him into big trouble. In the past, when he flew into one of his frequent rages, Andy was likely to throw furniture across the room, drive his fist through a wall, or punch somebody's lights out. A dozen years before his visit with me, he had spent time in jail for physically abusing his wife and kids. This man had been like a hand grenade with the pin pulled, ready to go off at the slightest provocation.

During another time of marital separation caused by Andy's violent anger, his pastor and church elders had confronted Andy's sinful behavior. Church discipline in accordance with Matthew 18:15-20 was initiated. Even though Andy was beginning to respond to the Lord's discipline, his wife and the church leadership felt that still more help was needed.

Clint, Andy's pastor, called me. "David, I'm at the end of my wits with Andy. We have prayed together on numerous occasions about his anger. I sense his genuine desire to change and find freedom. He has made much progress, but both he and I are fearful of the future. I have counseled him from Scripture, and he is involved in a men's accountability group. But I still sense a reservoir of rage just below the surface. Nothing seems to help. I'm afraid that one of these days Andy might hurt someone again. Will you please talk to him?" I said I would if Clint came along. He agreed.

When the two men walked in, Andy was noticeably irritated because Clint had insisted that he come. I sat down with this six-foot three-inch, 230-pound keg of dynamite and began to talk. "Andy, your pastor has filled me in on your background, and I have read about some of the things you have done. I rejoice with you in your recent confessions and appreciate your desire to find freedom from your anger. But I want to tell you something else I know about you. I know that underneath the anger and violence and rage that have ruled your life for so many years, you are really hurting."

Andy's face softened, as if the anger was being drained from him. I continued, "In fact, when I think about the magnitude of abuse that has poured out of your life, I'm convinced that there is an enormous amount of pain and hurt and fear inside you. That pain has probably been festering there a long time. And you have been dealing with it all alone."

When I said the word "alone," tears came to Andy's eyes.

I said, "You know the pain is in there, don't you, Andy?"

He nodded in agreement.

"Andy, just like God brought you to a point of confession over your sinful rage, he also wants to minister healing to you at the point of your pain. Would you like to begin ridding yourself of the pain and hurt and fear that have haunted you all these years?"

He nodded, and the tears started to roll down his cheeks.

"You know that your pastor loves you, don't you, Andy?"

He indicated that he did.

"Then I'm going to slip out of the room for a few minutes. The Bible states that God is the God of all comfort, and at times he desires to share with us some of his comfort through others. If you are willing, I'd like you to move over beside Clint and just begin telling him about your hurt, and let your pastor hurt with you. Would you be willing to do that?"

Andy said he would.

I prayed with him briefly and then left the room. During the twenty minutes that I was gone, Andy wept and poured out three decades of deep hurt. When I returned, Clint and big, tough Andy were on their knees embracing. They had just finished praying together.

At Clint's encouragement Andy told me part of his story. Running home one night because he was late, nine-year-old Andy took a shortcut through the park. Some men stepped out of the darkness and grabbed him. The men sexually abused the terrified boy, then let him go.

When Andy finally got home, he was filled with shame and self-condemnation. Feeling that the abuse was his own fault, he took his punishment for being late and never told his parents about the incident in the park. For thirty years Andy had carried his pain and shame alone, blaming himself for the humiliating abuse he had suffered. "None of it would have happened," he had told himself repeatedly, "if I had not been late."

Andy had suffered through this relational and emotional crisis for thirty years, alone and without comfort. His sinful rage was inexcusable, and yet in a brief encounter with God's comfort, additional victory and freedom had been realized. Andy rose from his knees that day with a great burden lifted and a new perspective on his life as a Christian.

There was still much healing ahead. This was only one step in his journey of healing, but it was a very important step. His wife later offered her tear-filled comfort, and Andy experienced even deeper sorrow over how he had hurt her and his children. The Great Physician had begun a good work in Andy and his family. The Lord faithfully completed that work. Today Andy and his wife are lay leaders in their church, leading a team of couples who help other couples and families battling to experience God's abundance in their marriages.

Andy is an example of those who lash out at others in response to their pain. We call this behavior *hurling*. Some people hurl their pain at others through sharp words, cutting sarcasm, or outbursts of physical or verbal abuse. Cupboard doors could get slammed shut. Pots, pans, or dishes may fly—sometimes aimed at the one considered to be the offender. Other people respond by acting out through manipulative games of punishment or withdrawal. Like Andy, when we hurl our pain, others often retreat from us in fear, and we are left to hurt alone.

Another common response to emotional pain is to *hide* it. Hiding or burying pain is no more a healthy solution than hurling. When you bury emotional pain, you are in fact burying it alive. It may remain dormant for a while, but at some point and in some way it will express itself, perhaps through addictive or compulsive behaviors or self-abuse. Andy's violent hurling of his pain was actually a result of hiding his pain as a child. Hidden pain may also take on more "socially acceptable" forms of expression, such as perfectionism, workaholism, or strong self-reliant behavior.

Hurling or hiding emotional pain leads to the same unhealthy, unproductive outcome in marriage: diminished intimacy. The challenge is to deal with inner pain in such a way that it results in emotional healing and prompts deepened intimacy between spouses. As God effects this healing through you for your spouse and through your spouse for you, you both become conduits of his presence here on earth.

## HEALING RESULTS IN ONENESS

For years my misplaced priorities kept me from being God's channel for ministering to Teresa's needs. And when by God's help I began to reorder my priorities and focus on the needs of my wife, things began to change. Teresa explains what happened from her perspective.

"There are two sides to every relationship. I am the other half that contributed to the desert that separated David and me. I was a bundle of unhealthy emotions and unproductive behavior. But David's actions, or lack of actions, were no excuse for my behavior. I, not David, am accountable before the Lord for my actions. For many years of our marriage I did not focus appropriately on giving to David or responding properly to my pain. Rather, I chose some very wrong and self-defeating behaviors.

"Feeling insecure, I tried to control everything and everyone, giving me a false sense of security and making the people around me feel miserable. Rather than make my marriage and husband my top priority, I made the children top priority. Sensing a lack of approval from David, I became 'Ms. Efficiency.' I had a place for everything, and I put everything—and everybody—in its place, hoping to find approval. But my controlling spirit only made it harder for people to approve of me.

"I also needed attention. In a twisted sort of way, I got David's attention by nagging him and presenting ultimatums. When he did not respond the way I wanted, I tended to become even more critical and negative toward him and the ministry.

"Not a pretty picture, is it? I was fast becoming a critical, negative, controlling person living a self-sufficient life and needing no one. But the world I created was a world of hurt. My selfish, self-defeating attitudes and actions shut David out of my life. The love I once had for my husband grew cold. I felt rejected, disconnected, and very alone.

*H*URLING *or hiding emotional pain leads to the same unhealthy, unproductive outcome in marriage: diminished intimacy.*

"God did not appear to me in a dream or send a prophet to set me straight. And he did not send a tragedy as a wake-up call. In his bountiful mercy, God simply yet powerfully displayed his love through David. Yes, I needed to seek forgiveness for my selfish attitudes, hurtful actions, and misplaced priorities. I needed reproof and correction. But what I received instead was irresistible, constraining love through my husband.

"When David got in touch with the heart of God and made me and the children his ministry priority, I was overwhelmed. He did not come to me with conditions like: 'If I meet your need for security, you must quit criticizing me' or 'If I show you more attention, you must be less controlling.' He just began loving me freely and unconditionally with the sensitive, caring, compassionate love he received freely from God."

## THE HEALTHY CHAIN REACTION OF HEALING

Exercising loving patterns of behavior through meeting Teresa's relational needs netted immediate results. As I began to focus on meeting her needs, it prompted a healthy domino effect.

For example, one day I sat down at my desk at the church office and wrote Teresa a short appreciation letter. Instead of giving it to her that evening, I put it in an envelope, stamped it, and dropped it in the mail. My little note read:

> *Dear Teresa,*
> *When I consider all the ways I have let you down, I'm sure glad God has given you a forgiving heart.*
> *Love, David*

The next day I drove home anxiously wondering if the letter had arrived. But Teresa said nothing about it. The next day went by, and still no mention of the letter. I said, "Teresa, did you bring in the mail today?"

She nodded, adding, "Are you expecting something?"

"Oh, no," I said, playing dumb. "I was just wondering."

On the third day I didn't have to wonder anymore. As I came through the door, Teresa met me with the note in her hand and tears of gratefulness in her eyes.

Here is how the chain reaction of meeting needs works as the Holy Spirit prompts Christlike living. We sometimes call this the law of the harvest, based on Galatians 6:7: "You will always reap what you sow!" (NLT). Don't be misled. Remember that you can't ignore God and get away with it. You will always reap what you sow! As you sow the good seed by meeting your spouse's intimacy needs, you will reap the harvest of healing and oneness in your marriage (see diagram on page 131).

1. **An intimacy need is met.** You meet intimacy needs by providing the appropriate comfort, attention, acceptance, appreciation, support, encouragement, affection, respect, security, and approval. My simple note of thankfulness to Teresa met her need for approval.

2. **A fulfilled need prompts truthful thinking.** God's promise in Proverbs 23:7 comes into play here: "As he thinks within himself, so he is." When Teresa read my note, she was prompted to think something like, *I must be loved. I am important.*

3. **Truthful thinking gives rise to positive feelings.** As Teresa considered that she was loved and important, she began to *feel* loved and important, and she also felt grateful for the approval I had expressed to her.

4. **Positive feelings are usually expressed in productive behavior.** Such behavior includes kindness, consideration, and giving to others. Teresa's affectionate greeting when I walked in the door was the by-product of how she thought and felt.

5. **Productive behavior results in positive outcomes.** The fruit of this healthy chain of events includes functional families, open communication, and intimate relationships. The more I apply myself to meet Teresa's needs, the deeper our oneness becomes. This

is how God's plan for loving relationships is fulfilled. Each partner receives abundantly from God and gives gratefully to the other, and intimacy is the result. And the end result is glory and honor to the One who created marriage. The diagram illustrates the positive results of meeting relational needs.

## TO GOD BE THE GLORY

Something mysteriously wonderful began to happen as our marriage relationship deepened. Naturally, we experienced the blessing of God in the richness of our love. But other people also began to notice the miracle unfolding in our relationship. First it was our own children. Next it was our close friends and members of our church family. You might think our kids would respond with something like, "Hey, what's going on with Mom and Dad? They aren't arguing like they used to." Or you might expect our friends to say, "Did you notice that David and Teresa are getting along better?" But the focus wasn't on us at all; it was on God.

The deepened oneness we were experiencing turned our children and others to God. Our kids became more interested in spiritual things and participated more enthusiastically during our family nights together. Our extended families sought input and encouragement from us. Our church ministry to others began to flourish.

What was happening? We are convinced that God's presence in our marriage was drawing the attention of others to himself. God receives glory when people are committed to loving relationships. When Jesus prayed for his disciples—which includes all of us—in John 17, he said, "I have given them the glory that you gave me, that they may be one as we are one: I in them and you in me. May they be brought to complete unity to let the world know that you sent me and have loved them even as you have loved me" (John 17:22-23, NIV).

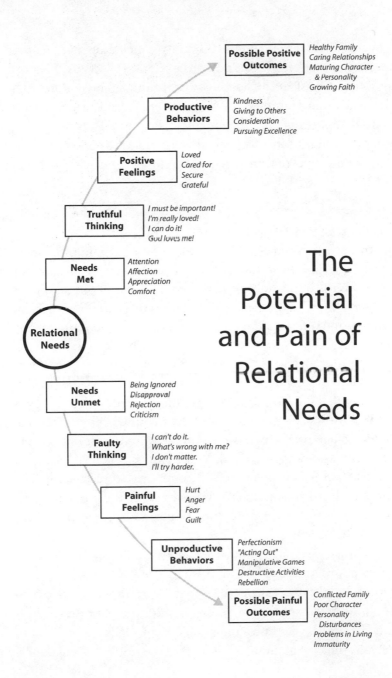

Possible Positive Outcomes
Healthy Family
Caring Relationships
Maturing Character
& Personality
Growing Faith

Productive Behaviors
Kindness
Giving to Others
Consideration
Pursuing Excellence

Positive Feelings
Loved
Cared for
Secure
Grateful

Truthful Thinking
I must be important!
I'm really loved!
I can do it!
God loves me!

Needs Met
Attention
Affection
Appreciation
Comfort

Relational Needs

The Potential and Pain of Relational Needs

Needs Unmet
Being Ignored
Disapproval
Rejection
Criticism

Faulty Thinking
I can't do it.
What's wrong with me?
I don't matter.
I'll try harder.

Painful Feelings
Hurt
Anger
Fear
Guilt

Unproductive Behaviors
Perfectionism
"Acting Out"
Manipulative Games
Destructive Activities
Rebellion

Possible Painful Outcomes
Conflicted Family
Poor Character
Personality
   Disturbances
Problems in Living
Immaturity

When Christians are bonded in unity—including marital oneness—God is glorified. Our unity as a couple reflects the oneness enjoyed by Christ and his Father—and it glorifies and honors God! This is a wonderful mystery. As your relationship deepens with your spouse, people are drawn to the heavenly Father. Dealing properly with hurt in a pain-filled world not only brings you and your spouse freedom, blessing, and intimacy, but God receives something as well: glory!

## WHERE DOES THE GLORY COME FROM?

Does it surprise you to know that you can be a conduit for God's glory in your marriage and that his glory in your relationship can actually turn people to him? It shouldn't. Throughout Scripture, God has chosen to display the glory of his presence to his human creation, and wherever his glory appeared, people were attracted to him. God's presence in your marriage, as he heals inner hurts through your loving ministry to each other, is one of the primary expressions of his glory in the world today.

One of the first Bible references to the glory of God is in the account of Moses and the bush that burned but was not consumed. God's presence was in that bush, and the wonder of it caused Moses to turn aside and seek God. We see God's glory a little later on Mount Sinai. After being in God's presence to receive the Ten Commandments, Moses' face radiated with the glory of God. And this phenomenon drew the attention of the people to the Word of God.

When Israel built the ark of the covenant according to God's specifications, the glory of God filled it. The glory in the ark actually directed the people from place to place, from provision to provision, from victory to victory. Israel was led and protected by a cloud of glory by day and a pillar of glory by night.

By the time of Solomon, the portable tabernacle was replaced by a beautiful temple as Israel's center of worship. When the ark was moved into the temple, the Lord's presence filled the place (see 1 Kings 8:1-11). "The cloud filled the house of the Lord, so that the priests could not stand to minister because of the cloud, for the glory of the Lord filled the house of the Lord" (verses 10-11). And God's presence called the people to worship.

But in the ensuing generations, Israel's leaders abandoned the truth of God's Word, and the nation fell into idolatry and immorality. Israel eventually divided into two kingdoms, and both kingdoms ended up in captivity. The people cried out to God, "Why are we in bondage?" The answer came though the prophet Ezekiel, who in a vision saw the glory of God leave the temple and ascend into heaven. A child was born in the priesthood at that time, and he was appropriately named Ichabod, meaning, "The glory has departed." The testimony of the prophets to the people was, "You are in bondage because the glory of God is gone."

For four hundred years between the Old and New Testaments, the priests went into the temple and performed their religious rituals, but the glory was not there. No wonder the first century opens with people in bondage to legalism. Then, one night on a hillside in Judea, angels appeared to shepherds and "the glory of the Lord shone around them" (Luke 2:9). What was happening? The glory was about to come back!

*GOD'S presence in your marriage, as he heals inner hurts through your loving ministry to each other, is one of the primary expressions of his glory in the world today.*

Christ was born, grew up, and began his ministry. John wrote of him, "The Word became flesh, and dwelt among us, and we beheld His glory" (John 1:14). For thirty-three years the presence of God was again on earth, not in an ark, not in a temple, but in a person. And this person, who knew no sin, became sin for us, was crucified, and then rose again. At Christ's ascension, the glory again departed the earth and returned to heaven.

Ten days later, on the Day of Pentecost, Christ's followers heard the sound of a mighty, rushing wind and saw tongues of fire—reminiscent of the fiery pillar of God's glory in the Old Testament. What was happening? The glory was back again, but in a brand-new way, which Paul called a mystery: "Christ in you, the hope of glory" (Col. 1:27). The presence and glory of God, in the person of the Holy Spirit, now resides in Christ's body, the church.

This brings new significance to Paul's familiar words in Philippians 4:19: "My God shall supply all your needs according to His riches in glory in Christ Jesus." Who meets all our needs? Our God. How does he meet those needs? Through the riches of his glory. But where is that glory? *It's in you and your spouse!* As you lovingly minister to each other, God is present and his glory is made known.

Is your marriage an expression of God's glory? Are you God's instrument for meeting each other's needs and healing each other's hurts? When your children and others observe your marriage, are they captivated by what they see and encouraged to seek God as a result? Do they ask where you get that love you share with each other? Are they motivated to pay attention to the Word because of God's presence in your relationship?

God is looking for an expression of his presence in your relationship. As you lovingly serve and care for one another, you are a conduit of his glory. As a result, you are able to meet each other's needs, heal each other's hurts, nurture intimacy, and help turn others toward God and his Word. Could marriage be any better than that?

# CHAPTER 8

# The Glory of Hurts Being Healed

I t was my birthday, so Teresa had invited our extended family over for barbecued steaks. On occasions like this, Teresa slips into a special gear that I humorously refer to as "whip and drive." She puts her mind to getting things organized and getting people fed in the most efficient way possible.

With Teresa humming along in whip-and-drive mode for my birthday dinner, I got the big idea that I could help. This was a break from tradition around our house because I don't cook. But that day I boldly swaggered into the kitchen where everybody was hanging out and announced, "I'll barbecue the steaks." And since I viewed gourmet homemade barbecue sauce as a "guy thing," I started messing around with the bowl of sauce that was already mixed and ready to go.

When Ms. Efficiency saw what was happening, she came unglued. "David, what do you think you're doing?" Teresa barked in front of everyone. "Leave the barbecue sauce alone, or you'll spoil it."

Her words could not have hurt more if she had jabbed me with a knife as she spoke them. "Then just forget it," I snapped defensively. I tossed the meat fork down and stomped out of the kitchen.

Not only had Teresa embarrassed me in front of our family, but her reaction to my interference had ripped off a scab from unhealed pain left over from my childhood. My father was a no-nonsense marine drill sergeant, and he seemed just as tough at home. If Dad couldn't make a quarter bounce off my bed in the morning, I had to keep making it until he could. Even with good motives to see me disciplined and diligent, he was a hard man to please at times.

As a boy I yearned for the closeness and affection that Dad seemed unable to show. Whenever he worked on our car, I would go into the garage just to be near him. Sometimes he would bark an order like, "Son, give me the half-inch socket." The problem was, I wasn't all that familiar with tools. So in my effort to please, I might hand Dad an open-end wrench instead. If it was the wrong tool— and it often was—he might throw it down, curse, and order me into the house. These occasions of rejection hurt me deeply. And any time Teresa might criticize me in areas where I felt inadequate, the old, unhealed pain came back to haunt me again.

My painful birthday experience is an example of the way unhealed hurts from the past can become a hindrance to intimacy in a marriage relationship. True, Teresa was wrong to criticize me in front of the family, and she quickly realized her mistake and addressed it. But the deeper issue at hand was the long-standing pain she had uncovered from my past, pain she had not caused. When these deep hurts in you or your spouse are not healed, the oneness you long for in marriage will continue to elude you.

## COMFORT—GOD'S REMEDY FOR PAIN

When you or your spouse come into contact with pain you did not cause—whether it be from the past or the present—you have three choices. First, you can hide the pain by ignoring it and whatever brought it up. But it will still be there, and it will come back to hurt you again and again while hindering intimacy in your relationship.

Second, you can hurl the pain as I did when I snapped at Teresa, threw down the meat fork, and stormed out of the kitchen.

Hurling our pain doesn't get rid of it, and it will likely compound the pain in your relationship.

Third, you can pursue healing for your pain, thus experiencing greater intimacy and becoming a conduit for God's glory in your relationship. This is God's provision for your pain. He desires to involve each of you to minister to the pain and provide the healing of comfort.

In the Sermon on the Mount, Jesus said, "Blessed are those who mourn, for they will be comforted" (Matt. 5:4, NIV). Comfort is God's remedy for the dark, disappointing, and painful moments of life we all experience. Comfort is God's solution for easing the pain and healing the inner hurt caused by life's troubles. But he yearns to share his healing comfort through each of us.

In 2 Corinthians 1:3-4, Paul describes God as the "God of all comfort; who comforts us in all our affliction so that we may be able to comfort those who are in any affliction with the comfort with which we ourselves are comforted by God." There is a measure of comfort only God can give, but there is also a measure of God's comfort that he is pleased to give others through us—and to give us through others. It is not that God's comfort is insufficient or ineffective. He is the "Father of compassion and the God of all comfort" (2 Cor. 1:3, NIV). He hurts with us and comforts us at a level only he can touch. But in the great mystery of his sovereignty, he has chosen to share a measure of his ministry of comfort through us.

So how does it happen? How does God's comfort expressed through you heal a measure of your spouse's pain and bring you closer together? It's not a clever three-step method or psychological technique. It is an aspect of the mystery of God involving you and your spouse in his healing process and receiving glory in the process.

*THERE is a measure of comfort only God can give, but there is also a measure of God's comfort that he is pleased to give others through us— and to give us through others.*

## EXPERIENCING THE GLORY OF HEALING

The healing of inner pain is the work of a loving God who desires to display the glory of healing through us. The healing power of comfort is a "God thing." Hurts are not healed on the basis of what we do but as a result of his healing presence as we minister to one another. And when comfort is provided and healing is experienced, we are moved to wonder, "Where did the healing love in my partner come from?" And we are drawn immediately to the God of all comfort, and he receives glory.

When Teresa realized that she had hurt me on my birthday, she quickly and compassionately responded. Here is her account of what happened after our scene in the kitchen.

"When David tossed down the meat fork, whirled, and left the room, I realized how deeply I had wounded him. Aware of David's painful childhood, I knew I had thoughtlessly touched an old wound. At that point, the birthday party and all my preparations were unimportant. The steaks could burn to embers and our guests could starve, but I had to make things right with my husband.

"I went into the living room where David was hurting and put my face close to his. Touching his arm, I said with remorse, 'David, I realize how I have just hurt you. I deeply regret the pain I have caused you. It was so wrong of me. Will you forgive me?' David said yes, and we embraced. I was reminded of the fact that just a momentary lapse in my sensitivity can deeply hurt the one I love most. But I was also keenly aware that God was at work through me to minister an additional measure of healing to David's hurt."

Later that evening after our guests were gone, Teresa and I sat down together and dealt with the pain behind my outburst. I explained how her critical remarks seemed to touch a deep sense of rejection and inadequacy in me. I was then able to identify an important unmet need related to the pain: "Teresa, so many times in my life I have not sensed loving affection, and it hurts deeply."

Teresa recalls, "When David told me about his lack of affection,

I got a picture of young David crying into his pillow over his sense of rejection. I also considered how God must have felt as he looked down on that little boy and saw him hurting alone. Feeling God's hurt for David heightened my own awareness of my husband's pain, and we wept together."

*T*HE *healing of inner pain is the work of a loving God who desires to display the glory of healing through us.*

As my wife became the instrument for God's comfort to me, the gentle words coming from her heart *sounded* something like this: "David, it deeply saddens me that you experienced such rejection in the past. I can only imagine the stab of hurt that must have pierced your heart that day in the garage and other times when you were rejected. I feel so sad that you had to experience that." There was also a certain *appearance* to God's comfort that day. It took the form of a warm embrace, the gentle stroke of her hand on my head, and tender tears flowing down her face.

As Teresa held me and wept with me, my hurt seemed to lessen. Teresa and I were acutely aware that something special was happening between us, something beyond the loving words, tender embrace, and tears. God was there in the room ministering his divine comfort through Teresa. As we recognized and acknowledged that God had brought a measure of healing to my pain through Teresa, he received glory and we experienced the glory of his presence. We began to understand what Jesus meant when he said, "Blessed are those who mourn, for they will be comforted" (Matt. 5:4, NIV). As I mourned my hurt and received God's comfort through my wife, we were indeed blessed!

The blessing of mourning and comforting each other's emotional hurts has become an ongoing discipline in our marriage. When Teresa and I experience the inevitable disappointments, misunderstandings, and rejections in life, we seek to become channels of God's comfort and glory for each other. We no longer keep disappointments to ourselves. We resist the self-reliant temptation to handle life's routine disappointments alone. We continually ask God to help us to resist the temptation to hurl or hide the pain. The results have been revolutionary for us as we have experienced the power of God's comfort and the glory of God's healing.

AN EXERCISE IN COMFORT

God wants to reveal his glory in your midst and deepen your intimacy as a couple by healing your hurts through one another. The following exercise will guide you. Complete the first three steps separately, writing your responses on a blank sheet of paper. Then select a time to come together with your sheets and complete the final steps.

1. **Identify your needs.** If you have not completed the Intimacy Needs Assessment Inventory in appendix A, take time to do that now.

2. **Reflect on your top needs.** In the Intimacy Needs Assessment Inventory, you identified your top needs. List your top three needs on your sheet.

3. **Select one unmet need.** Consider how one or more of these needs may have gone unmet, either recently or in the past, resulting in personal pain. Choose an incident of pain that was not caused by your spouse. It may be something such as an unfulfilled expectation at work, rejection by a friend, or significant disappointment at church. Describe the incident as completely as possible on your sheet.

4. **Share with your spouse.** When you come together, take turns sharing with each other what you wrote. Describe your sense of loss and pain to each other. Listen intently as your partner shares his or her hurt. Seek to capture God's heart of compassion for your spouse. How do you think God feels about the pain your spouse suffered? Imagine Christ being moved with compassion, wrapping

his arms around your spouse and hurting with him or her. Allow God's Spirit to prompt his comfort through you.

5. **Comfort your spouse.** Now allow God to involve you in his ministry of comforting each other. Allow his compassionate heart of sorrow to be expressed through yours. Allow his warm embrace to be expressed through yours. Allow his tender comfort to be expressed through words such as "I'm saddened by what happened to you"; "I'm sorry you had to experience that, because I care about you"; "I hurt for you."

Resist the temptation to counsel, correct, instruct, or fix the problem. Simply be God's channel of comfort. As you do, God's presence will be in your midst, and his ministry of healing will take place.

## EXHIBITING THE GLORY OF GIVING

A vital component for experiencing God's glory in your marriage is the grace of giving to your spouse. This truth was emphasized to me in our marriage as I began to learn more about the pain in Teresa's past and how it had affected her needs in the present.

One area my wife and I have clashed over repeatedly in our marriage is our traveling. Whenever we leave on a trip, Teresa insists that we get to the airport early, giving plenty of time to park and get to the gate a full hour before our scheduled departure. I take a much more casual approach, figuring that if the plane is supposed to leave at 9:00 A.M., we don't need to be there until 8:55 to walk on and sit down. To me, an hour lingering in the airport boarding area is an hour of productive time wasted. So every trip renewed this conflict. Teresa snaps into whip-and-drive mode to get us to the airport early, and I drag my feet,

*A vital component for experiencing God's glory in your marriage is the grace of giving to your spouse.*

knowing the plane won't leave without us—and if it does, there will be another one soon.

But as I began to learn about my wife in order to become more caringly involved in her life, I discovered a deep-seated fear from her childhood. Growing up in a large family of limited means, she feared at times that there might not be enough food for her. She feared there would not be enough money to meet her needs. Three of her five siblings were hearing impaired and attended special schools. These children got the new clothes, and Teresa got hand-me-downs, so she often feared there would not be enough clothes for her. She grew up in constant fear that there would not be enough of anything for her, and she struggled with this fear all alone.

Such fears no doubt contributed to Teresa's coming into adulthood with a high need for security. On the issue of traveling to the airport, her need might sound something like this: "We must get to the airport early because there may not be enough parking places. If we can't get into the main lot, we may have to park in the remote lot where we have to ride a shuttle bus to the terminal. If the shuttle is full, we may not get to the terminal to board on time, and there may not be enough room in the overhead compartment for our carry-on bags. And if we have to check our carry-ons, they may get lost and we won't have what we need when we arrive. So we have to get to the airport early."

For years I just argued with Teresa about what I regarded as her paranoid approach to travel. But all my logic did nothing to meet her need, and the unresolved conflict and pain hindered our intimacy.

As I began to welcome Christ as my colleague and companion in loving Teresa, God began to speak to me about this issue. Our dialogue might be characterized by something like this, based on what he was teaching me from Matthew 25:40:

Jesus: "I needed to get to the airport early, but you would not take me."

David: "Lord, when did you need to get to the airport early and I did not take you?"

Jesus: "Every time you ignored Teresa's need for security and failed to get her to the airport early, you did it to me."

God's convicting word to my heart produced a sense of brokenness. Not only had I hurt and disappointed my wife by failing to love her as she needed to be loved, I had hurt and disappointed the Savior. I began to see the issue differently. I wondered if my effort to get to the airport would not only bless my dearest one but in some mysterious way even bless our God. *This is the weirdest thing I have ever heard, God,* I thought. *We don't have to be at the airport so early. The plane won't leave without us. If our luggage gets lost, they will find it and deliver it to us. It's no big deal. But if this is the path to loving Teresa and blessing you, I guess I should head that way even though it seems like a waste of time.*

So we started leaving for the airport when Teresa wanted to leave. We were able to park, check in at the gate, and get our boarding passes in plenty of time. Teresa was thrilled, and I sensed God's pleasure in simply giving to meet her need. But as I sat down in the boarding area for up to an hour, at times it still felt as if I was wasting valuable ministry time.

But something glorious began to happen. God took those hours in the airport and began to transform them into some of the sweetest times of insight, wonder, and worship I have ever experienced. A great deal of the biblical revelation I have shared recently in conferences and training sessions came to me while sitting in airports. There was something wonderfully mysterious about it, as if the Lord was saying, "You thought this would be wasted time. But you gave of yourself to meet Teresa's need and to heal some of her childhood pain. And by allowing her more time at the airport, *you and I* have more time at the airport. By your glorifying me through giving, I let my glory overflow to you."

EXHIBITING THE GLORY OF UNCONDITIONAL LOVE

The glory of unconditional love is beautifully exemplified in Jesus' encounter with a tax collector. In fact, this encounter in Luke 19:1-10 so clearly pictures the impact of unconditional love that we often refer to it as the "Zacchaeus Principle."

As an agent of the Roman government, Zacchaeus—a Jew—reached deep into Jewish purses for Roman taxes. Whatever else he could extort from the people he likely kept for himself. The Jews typically regarded tax collectors with contempt, as deceitful traitors and thieves. His fellow citizens probably despised Zacchaeus, and he quite possibly felt rejected, guilty, fearful, and alone.

When Jesus came to town, Zacchaeus wanted to hear him speak. But because the tax collector was not very tall, he had trouble seeing Jesus. In a resourceful move Zacchaeus climbed up into a sycamore-fig tree, from where he could hear and see plainly. When Jesus passed the tree, he looked up, knowing all about the sinful behavior of the man peering down at him. It is notable, however, that Jesus did *not* say to him, "Zacchaeus, you lying, cheating thief, get down here right now and stop your sinful behavior." Rather, he said, "Zacchaeus, come down immediately. I must stay at your house today" (Luke 19:5, NIV). Jesus offered to enter the man's home and, as was the custom, eat out of the same dish with him. He could hardly do anything more accepting! Indeed, one of the Pharisees' big complaints was that Jesus actually ate with tax collectors and sinners.

Zacchaeus's immediate response demonstrated the impact of Jesus' offer: "He came down at once and welcomed him gladly" (v. 6, NIV). How thrilled he must have been that the popular, miracle-working rabbi wanted to be with him! Zacchaeus may have experienced the same satisfying fulfillment we all experience when our spouse or a friend or even a stranger ministers to us at a time of feeling alone. Teresa felt something like this when I began to respect her need for security by making sure we get to the airport early. This is the glory of giving exhibited.

Jesus did not ignore the fact that Zacchaeus was a lying, cheating thief who needed to love and obey God with heart, soul, and mind. Jesus verbalized his concern for Zacchaeus's sin later in the conversation: "The Son of Man came to seek and to save what was lost" (v. 10, NIV). Jesus sought Zacchaeus at a relational level, taking time out to visit with this lonely, rejected, insecure man. As a result, Zacchaeus's spiritual needs were addressed very naturally in the context of this relationship. Luke 19:8-9 says, "Zacchaeus stood up and said to the Lord, 'Look, Lord! Here and now I give half of my possessions to the poor, and if I have cheated anybody out of anything, I will pay back four times the amount.' Jesus said to him, 'Today salvation has come to this house, because this man, too, is a son of Abraham'" (NIV).

What happened in Jesus' incredible encounter with Zacchaeus? To paraphrase a popular song from several years back, Jesus looked beyond the man's fault and saw his need. And when the love of Christ gave to Zacchaeus at the point of his need, that love constrained the sinner to confess his sin and make things right. In other words, Christ's love ministered to the man's deep need, and Zacchaeus responded by allowing God to deal with his fault.

Your responsibility in ministering to your spouse is not to correct faults, even when those faults may be contributing to your partner's hurt. Your responsibility is to look beyond the faults, meet the apparent need, and be God's instrument of healing to any hurts. Any need to address "faults" can come later. As you lovingly give to your spouse, God's glory is exhibited in your midst to bless your partner, heal his or her hurts, and confront any issues that need to be dealt with.

## EXPRESSING THE GLORY OF FAITH

Duane sat directly across from me, fidgeting in his chair. At his wife's insistence, he had stayed with her after one of our leadership conferences to visit with us.

Kim began by sharing with us a list of ways Duane had been neglecting their relationship. It was obvious that Kim had been hurt, and she wasn't shy in letting her husband know it. She explained, "I do everything I can to show Duane how insensitive and uncaring he is to me."

"Now Kim," Duane countered, "I care for you very much. I just don't do everything to your liking, that's all." He directed his next words to Teresa and me. "I just can't live up to her expectations. When she is struggling with something, she looks to me for the comfort and encouragement she needs. I try, but I always seem to fall short in the emotional support department."

I turned to Kim. "When you are down emotionally and go to Duane for help, what do you say to him and what does he do?"

"Well," she began, "I tell him how I'm feeling, and he just doesn't respond to me. He knows I'm hurting, and he doesn't care."

"Then what do you do?" I probed.

"What do you mean?"

"I mean, when you are emotionally hurting and your husband isn't there for you, how do you respond?"

"It sort of builds up inside, and I eventually blow up," Kim said. "I let him know that he's not being a very supportive husband to me."

Turning toward Duane, I said, "And how do you respond to that?"

Duane shrugged. "I tell Kim that I don't know what more she wants from me. I can never seem to do enough for her, no matter what I do."

Both Kim and Duane had valid needs that God desired to meet and painful hurts that God desired to heal. And he wanted to minister to each of them through the other, but it clearly wasn't happening. This dilemma is played out in most couples at some time or another. What are we to do when, for whatever reason, we are hurting and our spouse is not there to minister to our needs and hurts in a timely and effective manner?

We must always remember that God is the ultimate provider of everything we need. It is true that he channels a measure of his provision through others such as our spouses, but that doesn't limit him or his provisions. He has promised to "supply all your needs according to His riches in glory in Christ Jesus" (Phil. 4:19). God will always keep his promise even when your spouse is unable or unwilling to keep his or her promises to meet your needs.

So what are you to do when your spouse is not cooperating with God's desire to meet some of your needs? Words from the apostle Peter provide an answer: "Above all, keep fervent in your love for one another, because love covers a multitude of sins. Be hospitable to one another without complaint. As each one has received a special gift, employ it in serving one another, as good stewards of the manifold grace of God. . . . Whoever serves, let him do so as by the strength which God supplies; so that in all things God may be glorified through Jesus Christ. . . . If anyone suffers as a Christian, let him not feel ashamed, but in that name let him glorify God. . . . Therefore, let those also who suffer according to the will of God entrust their souls to a faithful Creator in doing what is right" (1 Pet. 4:8-11, 16, 19).

This passage explains how to respond to trying experiences, which include a marriage relationship in which some needs are not being met. If you are in such a situation, these words encourage you to

- remain fervent in your deep love for your partner;
- remain hospitable (pleasant and receptive) to one another without complaining;
- continue to serve one another;
- not be ashamed that you are struggling in this area;
- exercise your faith in God to meet your needs in his own way.

It is not easy to continue to express love toward your spouse in these ways when you are suffering from unmet needs. The key to experiencing this passage is found in giving first and putting your faith in God's trustworthy character and his promise to be your provider. You must look beyond your partner's fault to see his or her need and give to meet that need. As you give to your spouse, even when you are in need and hurting, you become a conduit for God's glory in your relationship. The glory of faith is expressed. God comes on the scene to meet your needs and to deepen intimacy with your partner.

In the Sermon on the Mount, Jesus admonishes us to love those who hate us, to turn the other cheek, and to give to those who only want to take from us. Jesus concludes by promising, "Give, and it will be given to you; good measure, pressed down, shaken together, running over, they will pour into your lap. For by your standard of measure it will be measured to you in return" (Luke 6:38).

Do you see the significance of giving to meet the needs of an uncooperative spouse? Is Jesus actually saying that as you selflessly meet your partner's needs, your needs will be met in return? We definitely believe so. We sense Christ saying, "Give to your spouse first from a servant's heart without expecting anything from your partner in return, and I will see to it that your needs are met . . . in whatever way I might choose." When you give to your resistant spouse, your faith is strengthened, and that pleases God (see Hebrews 11:6). But then God also works to honor his promise to bless you.

## WHAT SHOULD BE OUR EXPECTATIONS?

Kim expected Duane to be a sensitive, caring husband and follow through on his commitment to meet her needs. She certainly did not consider these expectations to be unreasonable, especially since she made it very clear to him where he was falling short. So it was difficult for her to hear us say that she needed to keep loving Duane and meeting his needs and trust God to meet her needs. This challenge became even more difficult in the ensuing months when Kim found out that Duane was having an affair. He subsequently separated from her.

The pain of Kim's unmet needs due to Duane's neglect was bad enough, but the betrayal of his unfaithfulness was almost unbearable for her. Yet she was committed to stay yoked with Christ in her marriage even though Duane was not with her. We explained to Kim that Christ had also experienced betrayal and modeled for us a loving response: "For you have been called for this purpose, since Christ also suffered for you, leaving you an example for you to follow in His steps, who committed no sin, nor was any deceit found in His mouth; and while being reviled, He did not revile in return; while suffering, He uttered no threats, but kept entrusting Himself to Him who judges righteously" (1 Pet. 2:21-23).

*As you give to your spouse, even when you are in need and hurting, you become a conduit for God's glory in your relationship.*

Christ did not strike back in bitterness and resentment even though he suffered unjustly. But neither were his persecutors let off the hook when Christ continued to love them despite their mistreatment. Jesus placed his expectations in his Father and kept entrusting himself to him who judges righteously. Christ left the unjust in the hands of the just judge and continued to love. You must do the same. Your spouse is not let off the hook when you turn your expectations to God and continue to love your spouse. God will deal justly with your spouse in his good time.

In the meantime, continue to direct your expectations to God and trust him to fulfill your needs in his way. This is the invitation of 1 Peter 5:6-7: "Humble yourselves under the mighty power of God, and in his good time he will honor you. Give all your worries and cares to God, for he cares about what happens to you" (NLT). Entrusting your needs to God may require that you patiently endure the pain of unmet needs for a time. But God will be there to minister to you through his Word, through prayer, and through the power of his Holy Spirit. He may also direct his need-meeting presence to you through a dear friend, another family member, or members of your church family.

During her trying time apart from Duane, Kim turned to her father and mother, whom God used powerfully to meet her needs for comfort and security. She eventually joined a "Restoring Intimacy" group at one of the Great Commandment Ministry churches. Kim met others in the group whose marriages were also in pain, and God involved these people in meeting her needs, especially for encouragement and support.

As the group focused on biblical principles for saving a marriage even when a spouse is not cooperating, Kim discovered liberating insights. She was convicted of her own selfishness and critical spirit toward Duane. She began to understand his pain and needs. Little by little, God began to restore their marriage. Today Duane and Kim help lead marriage ministry groups in their church.

God desires glory out of your marriage: the glory of giving to meet needs, the glory of unconditional love, and the glory of faith. But even if you are struggling and discouraged in your marriage because your needs are not being fully met, God can still receive glory in your marriage when you glorify him in the midst of your troubles. As you lift up your heart to give thanks, praise, and adoration to God even when your marriage is less than you desire, he is glorified. And the more you express gratitude and praise for his faithfulness, caring love, compassion, and power, the more your faith will increase and be strengthened.

# CHAPTER 9

# Your Role in the Healing Process

We know that relational hurts in life are inevitable. We also know that comfort is God's healing remedy for that pain and that he desires to involve us in the healing process with our spouses. But what happens when your partner's pain is partly your fault because of something you said, did, or failed to say or do? Can you still be a conduit for God's glory in the healing process when you have significantly contributed to the pain?

Yes, God is still very interested in ministering his healing through you, even though your self-centeredness, self-reliance, or self-condemnation has hurt your spouse. But the process becomes more complicated, not because your sin has made God's comfort less effectual, but because something fundamental must take place before you provide the needed comfort. I had to grasp this truth before I could effectively comfort Teresa for the pain I had added to her life.

As you might expect, my years of neglect and misplaced priorities had brought pain to Teresa and our children. Yet I seemed to be blind to the pain I had contributed. Yes, I knew that something was wrong whenever I heard a burst of angry words from Teresa or saw her tears. I would respond to her expressions by saying, "I'm sorry." I figured that my verbalized regret should have comforted Teresa and brought healing. But it did not because a fundamental ingredient was missing from my apology: true repentance.

I was not truly repentant because I failed to understand the magnitude of the pain I had contributed. Consequently, what little repentance I did express was shallow, and I easily became a repeat offender. Until we grasp more fully how we have hurt our spouses and the Lord, God's work of repentance in our lives will be hindered, and we are likely to keep on repeating the pain and hindering oneness.

UNDERSTANDING GOD'S PAIN

It was many years before the pain I added to Teresa's life on our honeymoon was fully healed. I had left Teresa sleeping in the motel room the morning after our wedding night while I went off to shoot pool with my buddy. Teresa walked home to her parents that morning feeling confused, alone, betrayed, unloved, and abandoned. This was major pain for her. For all she knew, I had left for California on a whim with my buddies, an irresponsible stunt I had pulled on my parents about a year earlier. Suddenly I was gone again, and Teresa had no way of knowing whether she would ever see me again.

When I finally showed up at her parents' house and found her crying, I knew I had blown it. I said something like, "I shouldn't have done that. Now let's go." I displayed about as much depth of understanding for her pain and sympathy as I would ordering a pizza. I kind of confessed my offense, and she kind of forgave me. And that's where the issue lay buried for the next fifteen years. My numbness to the magnitude of Teresa's pain contributed to a lack of intimacy from day one of our marriage.

After I became a Christian, I addressed the issue again. I think I said something like, "That was *really* wrong of me to go off to shoot pool that morning. Please forgive me." Still, I had not connected with the depth of her pain, so the issue was buried again for several more years. It wasn't until that Monday morning when I sat impatiently in the car waiting for Teresa that God began to get through to me. It was as if my insensitive behavior had built up, and I was beginning to feel guilty.

When I got to my office that Monday morning, God began to reveal to me how my self-centeredness had rendered me painfully insensitive to the very people I claimed to love. I needed to confess my sin in accordance with 1 John 1:9: "If we confess our sins, He is faithful and righteous to forgive us our sins and to cleanse us from all unrighteousness." I had preached on this verse many times. I had studied the word *confession* in the Greek. I knew it meant to agree with God about my behavior. So I started down the path of confession intellectually and theologically.

I prayed, "God, I agree that my actions were wrong and sinful. I agree that I was selfish." As usual, I was misapplying biblical truth. My confession was stuck up in my head. It was not going to work unless it got to my heart.

It was as if God said, "You *understand* confession intellectually, but you need to *experience* 1 John 1:9 personally. Not only do you need to agree that your self-centeredness is wrong, but you also need to know experientially what it has done to those you love. And you need to know that your selfishness is part of what sent my Son to the cross. If you really want to agree with me about your sinfulness, you must agree that it is part of why my Son had to die."

That truth pierced me like an arrow through the heart. The words of Isaiah 53 suddenly flooded my heart. It was as if the Lord was saying, "David, my Son was pierced and crushed because of your selfishness. The punishment your selfishness deserved was taken by him." Sitting in my office, I began to weep. My heart was broken

*UNTIL we grasp more fully how we have hurt our spouses and the Lord, God's work of repentance in our lives will be hindered, and we are likely to keep on repeating the pain and hindering oneness.*

like never before. That day God took me beyond simply acknowledging that my self-centeredness was wrong. He took me to the place of a broken, contrite heart and a godly sorrow. For the first time I was experiencing 2 Corinthians 7:10: "Godly sorrow brings repentance" (NIV).

The sorrow that overcame me was not my sorrow; it was God's sorrow. Previously, I thought godly sorrow was a sorrow like God's sorrow. But that day God shared with me some of the sorrow he must have experienced as he heard his sinless Son cry out, "My God, my God, why have you forsaken me?" (Matt. 27:46, NIV). The tears I shed that day were prompted by the Father's sorrow over the death his Son had to die because of my selfishness.

For the first time in my life I was deeply grieved over my self-centeredness. I felt heartwrenching guilt over the pain my selfishness had brought to Jesus Christ, the Lamb of God, who was slain on my account. And I deeply grieved over the desert of neglect and hurt my selfishness had caused Teresa for more than fifteen years. My misplaced priorities had shut her out and alienated her from the loving husband she needed. I saw her alone and hurting. Great sorrow for Teresa rose in my heart, and I sensed her pain as never before. I wept over how I had failed to express God's love to her. Just as promised, godly sorrow was producing repentance.

My heart turned to my three precious children. I sensed their longing for a daddy's attention, approval, acceptance, and protection. God had touched my heart, and I yearned to meet the needs I had neglected for so many years. The Father had opened my eyes to the pain and aloneness my loved ones experienced. I sensed his forgiveness, and with it came gratitude and renewed hope. The tears streaming down my face were no longer tears of sorrow but tears of joy and gratitude—the joy of his promised cleansing and gratitude for his forgiveness. I was truly experiencing 1 John 1:9.

## UNDERSTANDING YOUR SPOUSE'S PAIN

The impact of this time of brokenness in my church office was immediate. I went home to Teresa in the middle of the day and tearfully confessed not only my selfish behavior in the driveway that morning, but a pattern of self-centeredness that had painfully stolen from her my attention and care for more than fifteen years. A ministry of healing in our marriage began that day as the promise of James 5:16 was experienced: "Confess your sins to each other and pray for each other so that you may be healed" (NIV).

I knew that Teresa's honeymoon pain was still an unresolved issue between us. And so, more than fifteen years after the event, I sat down with her, desiring to show respect and consideration for my wife and our need for deepened oneness.

Feeling a significant amount of anxiety, I said, "Teresa, I want you to tell me about the pain you felt that morning at the motel. Take as long as you need; I want to listen. I want to understand how deeply I hurt you that day."

When you approach your spouse like that, you are in effect taking off all your protective armor and dropping your guard. You are opening yourself up to truth and honesty that may be painful for you to hear. But exposing the depth of the pain you contributed is critical to the healing process, both for you and your spouse. First, the process of understanding your spouse's pain is for your benefit, to effect godly sorrow and a true repentance that will minimize repeat offenses. Second, as you mourn with your spouse over the magnitude of the pain, God can prompt in him or her both deepened forgiveness and freedom from fear.

Teresa talked for almost a half hour— which seemed to me like four hours. God's

*THE process of understanding your spouse's pain is for your benefit, to effect godly sorrow and a true repentance that will minimize repeat offenses.*

work in her heart allowed her to express her feelings with "I" messages instead of accusing "you" messages.

"When I woke up all alone," she said, "I felt so betrayed and afraid. I sensed such deep rejection that I began to question my importance to you or to anyone."

As she described in detail the betrayal, fear, uncertainty, and hurt she felt, my heart broke again. I saw that confused sixteen-year-old girl walking home to her parents feeling used, abused, and abandoned. I sensed God's heart breaking for his beloved child whom I had wounded through my self-centeredness.

Teresa and I wept that day over the suffering I had caused. With new understanding and a contrite heart, broken now to the depth of her pain, I said, "Teresa, I am so sad for the pain I caused you. It hurts me deeply that you hurt like that. Will you forgive me?"

Her reply was powerfully reassuring: "I did that years ago, but it means so much to me that you care about my hurt." Our marriage experienced a new measure of intimacy as a fifteen-year-old incident was bathed in tears of true repentance and the blessing of genuine comfort.

### REWARDING STEPS TOWARD HEALING

The process of dealing with the hurts you have contributed to in your spouse is not easy. It is never easy to own up to wrongs you have done. But the outcome of deepened intimacy is worth the difficulty and discomfort of the process. Here are four rewarding steps toward healing.

**1. Invite your spouse to share his or her pain.** It is not pleasant to hear how your attitudes and actions have hurt your spouse, so it won't feel natural for you to confront him or her as I did that Monday. We suggest that you first talk to your spouse in principle, separate from any recent incident, about your desire to be God's channel of healing. You may say something like, "Honey, I know that from time to time I say or do things that hurt you. When I hurt you, I know I don't understand the depth of your inner pain. But because I want to keep from hurting you, I really want you to tell me just how deeply I hurt you. Will you agree to share that with me?" Giving your spouse permission to share his or her deep pain establishes that you are committed to intimacy in your relationship.

**2. Identify how God hurts for your spouse.** When you become aware of your spouse's hurt, God will be at work in you to give you his perspective of the pain. When your spouse shares the depth of his or her pain, a part of you will not want to hear it. The more you understand what you have done, the more convicted and uncomfortable you will feel about it. Your guilt and sorrow over what you have done will tend to override your sense of remorse and sorrow for your spouse's hurt.

I have found it helpful to detach myself for the moment from the fact that I had anything to do with Teresa's pain and focus on how God must hurt for her. It is almost as if Teresa is sharing with God how she has been hurt and I am observing God's brokenness over the suffering of his dear child. As you do this, listen to how your spouse has been hurt and try to sense how a compassionate, caring God hurts for her or him.

**3. Accept responsibility for your sin.** Own up to the fact that your sin has hurt your spouse and brought sorrow to God. God not only experiences sorrow over the hurt you have contributed to in your spouse, he feels sorrow over what your sin caused his Son to go through.

**4. Embrace God's sorrow as your own.** Experiencing God's sorrow and embracing it as your own is what brings forth repentance according to 2 Corinthians 7:10. Such sorrow prepares your heart for meaningful confession.

AN EXERCISE IN GODLY SORROW

You probably didn't abandon your spouse on your honeymoon as I did. You may not have struggled with critical or controlling behaviors as Teresa did. You may not need to confess a truckload of hurts inflicted on your spouse over a period of years as we have. But God may be putting his finger on some misplaced priorities in your life that have hurt your spouse. And self-centeredness, self-reliance, or self-condemnation may be at the heart of your misplaced priorities.

Allow the following questions to help you identify and evaluate how you may have hurt the person you love most. These questions correspond to the top ten intimacy needs discussed earlier in this book. Consider each question for a few minutes and allow God to bring to mind any ways you may have contributed to the pain of your spouse. Note the areas you need to confess to God and to your spouse.

1. How have I been insensitive to my partner's struggles instead of offering comfort?
2. How have I been oblivious to my partner instead of giving attention?
3. How have I communicated rejection to my partner instead of acceptance?
4. How have I expressed criticism instead of appreciation?
5. How have I neglected my spouse's burdens instead of providing support?
6. How have I prompted discouragement instead of encouragement?
7. How have I been cold or distant instead of displaying affection?
8. How have I been disrespectful of my spouse instead of demonstrating respect?
9. How have I prompted anxiety or fear in my spouse instead of providing security?
10. How have I displayed disapproval instead of approval?

As you reflect on any shortcomings suggested by these questions, allow God to search your heart and your motives. Allow him to show you how your sin has affected him and your partner. Open yourself to experience godly sorrow, and allow that sorrow to lead you into true repentance.

Ask God to bring sorrow to your heart over the ways you have hurt your spouse. Tell him you want to experience his sorrow, which leads to repentance. Allow yourself to experience the pain your heavenly Father feels for what your sin has caused. Hear the pain-filled words of your Savior: "My God, my God, why have you forsaken me?" (Matt. 27:46, NIV). Imagine the heartwrenching ache in the heart of the Father as he turned away while his Son became sin and suffered death alone for you.

*ASK God to bring sorrow to your heart over the ways you have hurt your spouse.*

Pause to express your heart's response to God. Ask the Father to soften your heart as he leads you into genuine confession.

Next, focus on how God must feel toward your wounded spouse. Has your involvement in activities, work, raising the children, or ministry—noble as these efforts may be—caused you to neglect your partner in some way? Have you been rejecting, insensitive, or unforgiving? How have these attitudes and actions made your spouse feel: Alone? Abandoned? Insecure? Afraid? Rejected? Now imagine the heavenly Father's compassion for your partner. Envision him wrapping arms of love around your spouse to comfort him or her and remove aloneness. He draws your loved one to himself to bolster security, to cast out fear, to comfort, to convey acceptance and love.

Sense God's desire to love your spouse through *your* heart of compassion, *your* loving words, and *your* caring deeds. Ask God to open your eyes to the pain and aloneness your spouse has experienced. Tell him you want to be an ambassador of his love to meet your partner's need and longing for intimacy.

AN EXERCISE IN CONFESSION

Take time now to experience 1 John 1:9 as guided by the following prayer. Write your personalizations on a separate sheet of paper or on the lines provided:

> *Heavenly Father, I realize that Jesus was wounded, bruised, and crushed for my sins against him and against my spouse. I am painfully aware of my misplaced priorities, self-centeredness, self-reliance, and self-condemnation. Specifically, I have hurt my spouse by*

_____

_____

> *Because of my sin, Christ died in my place and you heard your Son cry out, "My God, my God, why have you forsaken me?" As I contemplate your suffering for me, I feel _____. I have been wrong. I have hurt both you and my spouse. Forgive me. Fill me with gratefulness for your promised forgiveness and cleansing. Thank you, Father.*

AN EXERCISE IN HEALING HURTS

The following exercise is provided to help you experience James 5:16 with your spouse: "Confess your sins to each other and pray for each other so that you may be healed" (NLT). Each of you complete the first step separately on sheets of paper, then come together for the next two steps.

1. List the ways in which you have hurt your spouse and your marriage. For example, you may want to say you have been selfish, critical, negative, insensitive, disrespectful, ungrateful, or unforgiving. Your statements here should reflect issues that have caused sorrow to God's heart and yours._____

_____

_____

2. When you come together, share your lists with each other and request forgiveness. Husbands, you begin. As you hear your wife's confession, remember that forgiveness is a choice, not a feeling. The question is not "Do you feel like forgiving me?" but "Will you forgive me and let go of the hurt?" Good feelings follow right choices. Use the following dialogue, if necessary, to guide your interaction:

You: "I have seen that I have hurt you deeply by being _____. I have been wrong. Will you forgive me?"

Your spouse: "Yes, I forgive you."

You: "Are there other major hurts I am not aware of that need my apology? Please share them with me so that I can confess them now and ask your forgiveness."

After the husband has confessed his wrong, apologized, and received forgiveness, the wife can use the same dialogue.

3. Exchange your lists and tear them up or burn them. This act is an experience of Philippians 3:13: "Forgetting what lies behind and reaching forward to what lies ahead." Start the forgetting process by focusing on the new memory of forgiveness as lists are exchanged and destroyed. Then you may wish to hold hands and pray (even silently), thanking God for forgiving you, changing you, and healing your marriage.

## THE MOTIVATION BEHIND CONFESSION, FORGIVENESS, AND HEALING

All you need to do to find the motivation to follow through with the steps that lead to healing and intimacy in your marriage is look at the Father's heart. Not only is his heart touched with compassion for you and your spouse when you hurt, but his heart is also filled with joy when you become conduits of his glory by confessing your wrongs to each other, receiving forgiveness, and embracing his healing.

No passage in Scripture better describes God's joy over us than Jesus' parable of the Prodigal Son recounted in Luke 15. The story opens, "A certain man had two sons; and the younger of them said to his father, 'Father, give me the share of the estate that falls to me' " (verses 11-12). How would you have responded if you were the father? You might have said something like, "But, Son, don't take your inheritance and leave me. You have everything you need right here. Your selfishness will not bring lasting satisfaction. Rather, stay with me and enjoy what I have given you here." If the father objected in this way, it was to no avail. The son took his share of the estate and "went on a journey into a distant country, and there he squandered his estate with loose living" (v. 13).

The young man selfishly took his inheritance and in proud self-reliance went off to do his own thing. Can you hear him boasting to his new friends? "A brother? Yes, I have a brother who is a daddy's boy. He hasn't grown up yet. You have to be a real man to make it on your own these days. And I'm a real man!"

After the son had spent everything, a severe famine swept the country. Perhaps for the first time, the son began to feel in need. He ended up not only feeding swine but also eating from the feed trough himself just to survive.

Then he realized that even his father's servants back at home had more to eat than he had. He struggled with his unworthiness but finally decided to risk the journey. So he headed on the long road home. Can you picture him as the house comes into view in the distance? How did he feel about coming back to his father? Could he have been anxious and uncertain about the greeting he would receive? That's the way we feel when we realize that we have been selfish, proud, or down on ourselves. We come back to the Father, but we are wary of how he will respond to us.

Can you imagine the pain and sorrow the prodigal's father must have felt while his son was separated from him? It is a picture of the compassionate heart of God for us in our selfishness and sin. And while the prodigal was still a long way from the house, "his father saw him, and felt compassion for him, and ran and embraced him, and kissed him" (v. 20).

This is the picture that must burn into our hearts. As the prodigal walks up the dusty road toward the house, his father, who is waiting expectantly and longingly on the porch, sees him. The father, overcome with joy, scampers down off the porch and runs toward his son, arms outstretched. That is how your heavenly Father responds to you when you come in confession, needing forgiveness and healing. He is overjoyed, ready to embrace you, eager to restore you.

The faith he needed to replace his self-centeredness, the humility he needed to replace his self-reliance, and the gratefulness he needed to replace his self-condemnation would not come from what *he* did. This transformation could only come on the basis of what *his father* did.

When the boy delivers his self-condemning "I am no longer worthy" speech, the father ignores it. Instead, he turns to the servants and says, "Quickly bring out the best robe and put it on him, and put a ring on his hand and sandals on his feet; and bring the fattened calf, kill it, and let us eat and be merry; for this son of mine was dead, and has come to life again; he was lost, and has been found. And they began to be merry" (verses 22-24). A heart of joy compelled the father to leave the porch, race to his son, pronounce a relationship restored, and declare a celebration.

The prodigal must have been shocked by all of this. I can see him still kneeling before his father as a servant wraps a velvet robe around his shoulders. Another servant lifts up his hand and slips a jeweled ring on his finger while another provides sandals for his bare, travel-worn feet. The young man looks at the robe and the ring and the sandals in disbelief.

Then he lifts his head to gaze into his father's face. "Why, Father?" we can hear him ask. "Why do you do this for me?" It is a question you may be asking your heavenly Father. "Why are you so accepting of me in my failure to love my spouse as I should? How can your heart be so full of joy for me?"

We can hear the Father answer: "It is because of who I am. The more you come to know me, the more you will understand that I *must* rejoice when a relationship is restored and when intimacy is deepened. This is what I am about—turning the 'not good' of aloneness into the 'very good' of oneness."

It is a great mystery that an omnipotent, omniscient God grieves for you when your sin hurts you and your spouse, and then rejoices over you when you return to him. He doesn't require that you change your self-centeredness into faith before he throws a robe around your shoulders. He doesn't demand that you change your self-reliance to humility before he slips the ring on your finger. And he doesn't expect you to change your self-condemnation to gratefulness before he starts the celebration in your honor. He simply invites you to look to him and acknowledge that the power to be the loving husband or wife you want to be comes from him. And as you revel in the Father's unbounded joy over you, you will experience the faith, humility, and gratefulness that will transform you, heal the hurts in your marriage, and bring the oneness you long for.

> *G*OD simply invites you to look to him and acknowledge that the power to be the loving husband or wife you want to be comes from him.

PART
four

God's Community
We Share His Living Legacy

# CHAPTER 10

# Imparting Our Lives and Leaving a Legacy

Some time ago, Dave, a friend of ours, related in detail how he prepared and presented a living tribute to his seventy-five-year-old father, Harry. Dave wrote down what his father had meant to him during his growing-up years, listing many specific qualities his father had imparted to him as a legacy.

Dave had his written tribute professionally hand printed, bordered in gold leaf, mounted, and framed. Then, during a family gathering at which his own adult children were present, Dave read the tribute aloud to his father and gave him the framed copy. "It was a very moving experience," Dave said.

Here is a portion of Dave's tribute to his father.

*Dad, in one sense, your life in this world is coming to a close. But, in a true sense, your legacy will live on for generations because your very essence is very much alive within me and is being passed on to those who come after me. I can see your reflection in the mirror as I look at my own face. I can hear you in the inflection of my own voice. At times, I can feel you as I make a gesture or chuckle at something funny. Through the miracle of God's genetic master plan, you have passed on a part of yourself to me, and I have in turn passed it on to my son and my daughter. And with the birth of each passing generation, your "unique signature" will undoubtedly be seen and felt.*

*But more important, you have successfully passed to me*

*integrity, generosity, humor, a spirit of exploration, and caring for others. Because of your impact on me and your grandchildren, I see those qualities being carried on to the next generation.*

*You have been a loving and devoted father. And I will miss you so much when you are gone. But the life you have given me will live on. The qualities you instilled within me and the unique signature that I bear is your legacy. I have passed a part of you to my children. And my promise to you now is that I will teach my children's children of their heritage and of the qualities that have made you such a wonderful man. From generation to generation they will learn that the unique signature they feel within is from a man named Harry, son of John. You will live on and on and on. This, my solemn commitment to perpetuate your legacy to my children and their children, is my tribute to you.*

## IMPARTING OUR LIVES

Dave's father had become a living epistle to his family, imparting his very life to his son and instilling in him abiding qualities such as integrity, generosity, and a caring spirit. Dave was committed to perpetuate this legacy to his own children and grandchildren. The apostle Paul talks about this process in his letter to the Thessalonians: "Having thus a fond affection for you, we were well-pleased to impart to you not only the gospel of God but also our own lives, because you had become very dear to us" (1 Thess. 2:8).

When the living Word is experienced in our lives and our relationships, we are in fact imparting God's Word and our lives to others. As faith, humility, and gratefulness are perfected in us through God's abiding presence, we become living epistles of Christlikeness, imparting his living Word through our very lives to others. As you lovingly comfort your spouse, you are imparting God's Word and your life to him or her. As you lovingly meet your spouse's need for attention, you are imparting his Word and your very life to him or her. It is the same with each need you meet. And every time you impart his Word and your life to your spouse, God receives something very special from it: He receives a community of love and intimacy, a legacy to perpetuate his character to future generations.

This is a fourth response to the question posed at the opening of this book: What does God want out of your marriage?

First, God is looking for a *colleague* in the ministry of knowing and loving your spouse. When he receives in you and your spouse the colleagues he seeks, your longing to know and be known by each other will be fulfilled.

Second, God is looking for a *companion* in your marriage to meet your spouse's needs—and to minister to him in the process. When he receives in you and your spouse the companions he seeks, your longings to be cherished and to have your intimacy needs met will be fulfilled.

*W*HEN the living Word is experienced in our lives and our relationships, we are in fact imparting God's Word and our lives to others.

Third, God is looking for a *conduit* of his glory in your marriage, a vehicle to confirm his presence as he involves you in ministering to your spouse's inner hurts. When he receives in you and your spouse the conduits he seeks, your longings to be comforted and healed from life's inevitable hurts will be fulfilled.

Finally, God is looking for a *community* of love and intimacy that will transcend your relationship as husband and wife. When he receives in you, in your spouse, in your family—and beyond—the community he seeks, your longings to give yourselves to your loved ones without fear or reservation will be fulfilled.


## GOD GETS A FAMILY LEGACY

Dave described to us what happened after he read his tribute to his father. "Dad was deeply touched and in tears, and the rest of us were crying too," he said. "But what surprised me was the long-term effect my tribute had on him. About a month after our gathering, my mother reported that Dad would take the framed tribute off the wall every evening and sit down and reread it. Then, with tears streaming down his face, he would return it to the wall. Mom told me, 'Your tribute has given your father the greatest sense of accomplishment he has ever known.'"

Do you think God is blessed by the legacy of intimacy being perpetuated in Dave's family? Absolutely! And he is looking for this same legacy in your marriage and family. At best, you may live to see your legacy of love have an impact on three or four generations of your descendants. But our eternal God will receive glory and pleasure from your legacy through all of time and eternity! God receives an entire community of people imparting his Word through their lives. He is blessed not only by the oneness of your marriage but also by every succeeding generation that is influenced to oneness by the living epistle of intimacy in you. It is his living legacy!

Now consider God's disappointment when the legacy we perpetuate fails to accurately reflect him. Imagine how he must hurt when we fail to impart oneness and healing through our lives to the next generation. Our legacy of aloneness, unmet needs, and unhealed emotions may be passed on to generations to come (see Deuteronomy 5:9). Instead of presenting to God the ongoing community of joy and blessing, we hurt him by leaving a legacy of pain.

It is vitally important that you understand not only how to deepen intimacy between you and your spouse but also how to perpetuate that joyful legacy to your children. As my relationship with Teresa finally began to heal, I became painfully aware that I had been passing on a plague of emotional wounds to our three children. My insensitivity not only hurt my children, but it brought pain to God as I was denying him the community he sought.

## TRANSFORMING A PAIN-FILLED LEGACY

As our two daughters, Terri and Robin, were growing up, Teresa and I were in near perfect agreement about how to discipline them. But when our son, Eric, came along, we fell out of agreement because I just could not bring myself to tell him no. I was basically spoiling him. Teresa, on the other hand, made up for it by trying to nip his bad behavior in the bud. And the more she nipped him, the more I felt sorry for him and spoiled him. We ended up totally polarized about how to raise this little guy.

Ironically, at the same time that Teresa and I were struggling with our own parenting issues, we were expanding our ministry by teaching more parenting conferences for church leaders. One day Teresa said, "David, we have to stop teaching these conferences because we don't know what we're doing."

She was right. Eric was "acting out" in dramatic ways, and I did not yet realize that unresolved issues in my own life, especially issues related to my father, were provoking much of it. So for several years Teresa and I gave up our parenting conferences to concentrate on raising our own children.

At the age of eight, Eric was going through all kinds of anxiety, fear, and panic because of his parents' disunity over his behavior. His eating and sleeping habits were negatively affected. His stomach was tied up in knots. He refused at times to go to school and even tried running away from home.

Having learned about meeting needs in each other, Teresa and I went beyond trying to correct Eric's wrong behavior to discovering some of the causes behind it. In addition to administering appropriate and timely discipline, we also began to ask, "What does Eric need?" His anxious behavior told us he

*GOD is blessed not only by the oneness of your marriage but also by every succeeding generation that is influenced to oneness by the living epistle of intimacy in you.*

needed security. So we began to adjust our travel schedule to reduce our time away from him. When he complained about monsters in his room at night, we comforted him about his fears with compassionate reassurance and prayer instead of trying to explain them away rationally.

We began to enter his world, identify his needs, and experience God's Word with him at the point of his needs. The results were almost immediate. His sleeping and eating habits improved, and he began doing better in school. As his need for security was met, his anxiety was reduced. But a key element in Eric's lack of security was yet to be addressed.

Many people at this point would have said that our family was struggling with a problem child. I'm so thankful God protected us from those people. In reality, our family was struggling with a problem *dad*. My unwillingness to step up and discipline Eric was behind many of his problems. But a paralyzing fear from my past was at the root of my reluctance.

The issue came to a head one spring day when Eric was almost ten. It was clean-up-the-yard day at the Ferguson house, and everyone had an assignment. Eric's job was to dig up some dead plants in the front flower bed while the rest of us worked in the backyard. At one point I went around to the front yard to check on him. One dead plant had been dug up, but Eric was nowhere to be seen. He had hopped on his bike to go riding somewhere in the neighborhood.

Had Terri or Robin gone AWOL like that, I would have jumped in the car, tracked her down, disciplined her, and then stood over her until she completed her assignment. But this was Eric. So I quickly picked up the shovel and began digging up the dead plants, finishing his work for him. What's worse, I was not planning how I would discipline him when he got home. Instead, I remember thinking, *I had better hurry up and finish this job before Teresa catches me.*

In the counseling field, that's called pathological behavior: enabling my son's irresponsible behavior while fearing my wife will catch me doing it! And that day it struck me how unhealthy my behavior was, for both me and Eric. So with trepidation I began to explore what might be lurking behind my pathology.

I came face-to-face with a childhood fear that still controlled my behavior. It had never come out with my daughters, but it was coming out with my son. The fear sounded something like this: "If I discipline Eric, if I tell him no, I'm afraid he might not like me. I'm afraid he might feel toward me how I felt at times toward my dad, the rigid, drill-instructor disciplinarian from my childhood." This fear seemed to render me powerless to fully impart my life to my own son. The sad outcome of my unresolved fear was spilling out on Eric in many of the problems he experienced.

I knew I had to address the problem. First, I apologized to Teresa for my inconsistency and lack of support for her parenting efforts with Eric. Then I poured out to her my recent, painful realization of how the affection and approval I had often missed in my relationship with my dad was being expressed in a fear of losing Eric's affection and approval. I grieved, particularly over how my behavior was hurting Eric. Teresa mourned with me and comforted me as we prayed together. The Holy Spirit began to prompt Teresa to share a measure of God's affection and approval with me, ministering to needs I had missed as a child.

I then committed to join Teresa in meeting Eric's need for security through consistent discipline. I apologized to Eric for the hurt I had caused him by not providing guidelines and rules for his behavior. I even told him about my fear that he would not like me if I corrected him. And I promised that I would be more consistent at disciplining him. You can imagine how this commitment blessed him!

A few weeks later, I glimpsed God's grace at work as I followed through with my commitment. One morning as he was getting ready for school, Eric could not find the toothpaste in his bathroom. So he came into our bathroom and used the tube in our drawer. But instead of putting it away, Eric walked out, leaving the tube on the sink with the cap off. Now, this may not seem like a big deal to you. But having rarely disciplined Eric for the first ten years of his life, it was a big deal to me. I forced myself to call after him, "Eric, you need to come back and put the toothpaste in the drawer where you found it."

Much to my relief, Eric returned, screwed the cap on the tube, and put it in the drawer. As he left the bathroom this time, our quick-witted little guy looked back over his shoulder with a big smile on his face and said, "And, Dad, I still like you."

That morning I recognized the handiwork of a good God. He allowed me to experience Eric's affection and approval, assuring me that everything was going to be all right between my son and me. I hate to think what would have happened to him had I not dealt with my fear and the unmet need for approval from my past. Eric is now in his twenties and married to a precious wife, Katie, and the father-son bond between us has never been stronger.

IMPARTING YOUR LIFE TO YOUR CHILDREN:
AN ASSESSMENT
If you have children, imparting your life to them requires that you look for the needs behind their deeds, then move in to lovingly meet those needs. The following exercise will help you prepare to do that.

**1. Listen for needs.** Sensitive listening for needs is a critical element of compassionate parenting. Consider the statements below, and identify the underlying need: comfort, attention, acceptance, appreciation, support, encouragement, affection, respect, security, or approval. Then determine which of your children, if any, may at times make this type of statement:

|  | **Need** | **Child's name** |
|---|---|---|
| "You're too busy!" | _____ | _____ |
| "Look what I did!" | _____ | _____ |
| "I just can't do it!" | _____ | _____ |
| "I'm really upset!" | _____ | _____ |
| "I never get to choose!" | _____ | _____ |

**2. Give priority to family.** Occasions of uninterrupted family fun and togetherness provide a foundation for deeper relationships. Assess your time priorities, and write about specific plans for your family.

We can schedule regular "family nights" that could include:

_____

_____

_____

We can enter into each child's world—enjoying what he or she enjoys by:

_____

_____

_____

_____

We can develop these common interests and hobbies as a family:

_____

_____

_____

_____

**3. Affirm uniqueness.** Each child is uniquely special. Communicating and affirming each child's unique needs and qualities adds special blessing to the family.

Consider each child's unique intimacy needs: comfort, attention, acceptance, appreciation, support, encouragement, affection, respect, security, or approval. Then make plans to meet those needs.

| Child's Name | Needs | Plans to meet these needs |
| --- | --- | --- |
| _____ | _____ | _____ |
| _____ | _____ | _____ |
| _____ | _____ | _____ |
| _____ | _____ | _____ |
| _____ | _____ | _____ |

Consider each child's unique character qualities, such as sensitivity, diligence, dependability, creativity, compassion, flexibility, resourcefulness, and the like. Then plan specific ways you can affirm these qualities.

| Child's Name | Needs | Plans to affirm these qualities |
| --- | --- | --- |
| _____ | _____ | _____ |
| _____ | _____ | _____ |
| _____ | _____ | _____ |
| _____ | _____ | _____ |

**4. Heal hurts**. Prayerfully consider ways you may have hurt each child with your insensitivity to needs, wrong priorities, angry outbursts, disrespect, lack of support or compassion, and the like. Each hurt must be confessed, comforted, and healed.

| Child's Name | Specific hurts needing confession |
|---|---|
| _____ | _____ |
| _____ | _____ |
| _____ | _____ |
| _____ | _____ |
| _____ | _____ |
| _____ | _____ |

Now plan a time with each child to confess your wrong. Plan subsequent times to say something like, "Are there other ways I have hurt you? Please share them with me now and in the future. I want to confess any role I played in them. And I want to comfort you even if I did not play a role in the hurt."

**5. Impart your life**. Great blessing comes from imparting our lives to our children. Review the list of needs and qualities you identified under step 3. List at least one need you would like to meet and one quality you would like to affirm in your relationship with each child this next week.

| Child's Name | Needs | Quality to affirm |
|---|---|---|
| _____ | _____ | _____ |
| _____ | _____ | _____ |
| _____ | _____ | _____ |
| _____ | _____ | _____ |
| _____ | _____ | _____ |
| _____ | _____ | _____ |

As I discovered in my parenting of Eric, unresolved issues related to your own parents can be a major roadblock to intimacy with your children. What happened in your family of origin and how

177

you responded to it will either empower you to impart your life to your spouse and children or hinder that process. In the next chapter we will explore how to freely impart your life regardless of your family experiences and history.

# CHAPTER 11

# Leaving the Pain of the Past

The following statement may surprise or even shock you, but we know experientially and biblically that it is true: Unresolved emotional issues with your parents will hinder your intimacy with your spouse and limit your effectiveness in imparting your life to your children. How can conflict and aloneness from your family of origin so radically affect your own marriage and family? Teresa and I have already shared with you some of our story, how the unmet needs and unhealed emotions from our growing-up years hindered our intimacy with each other and with our children. Genesis 2:24 reveals a fundamental principle for relating to your family of origin and to your spouse and children: "A man shall leave his father and his mother, and shall cleave to his wife; and they shall become one flesh." Failing to follow the "leaving and cleaving" principle in your marriage will block your pursuit of intimacy and thwart God's desire to perpetuate his community through you.

*U*NRESOLVED *emotional issues with your parents will hinder your intimacy with your spouse and limit your effectiveness in imparting your life to your children.*

To cleave literally means "to be glued together." In a marriage relationship, it pictures a husband and wife becoming one, forming an enduring spiritual, emotional, and physical connection.

Leaving your father and mother means stepping free of any relational encumbrances and emotional baggage in your relationship with your parents. The implication of this verse is clear: Husband and wife cannot become one until they cleave to one another, and they cannot cleave to one another until they leave their father and mother. You and your spouse will not experience the depth of intimacy God has designed for you unless you unite spiritually, emotionally, and physically. And you cannot fully unite until you are free from any unhealthy attachments to father and mother.

The following scenario may help to underscore this principle. It's your wedding day, and the people who raised you are there for the event: a combination of parents, stepparents, grandparents, and/or guardians. The father of the bride (or another significant person in the family) escorts the bride down the aisle to the groom. As the ceremony progresses, your parents sit on either side of the aisle and beam with pride or brush away wistful tears. It is the public celebration of the two of you leaving your parents' homes to form a new family unit.

After the reception, you leave for the honeymoon. But as you climb into the limousine bound for the airport, both sets of parents are seated and waiting for you. When you board the plane for your honeymoon destination, they sit down right beside you. You check into your hotel room on your wedding night and, sure enough, your parents move right in to your room. And they stay with you wherever you go for the entire honeymoon. Not only is your privacy seriously compromised by their presence, but your unwelcome guests also badger you with a steady stream of parental instructions, directions, scolding, and discipline. You can't do anything or say anything without one of them coaching you, criticizing you, or complaining to you. How can you become one physically, emotionally, and spiritually under these nightmarish conditions?

In real life, no married couple would ever put up with such an arrangement. Yet scores of couples attending our conferences have experienced great conflict and aloneness in their marriages because their parents always seem to be "in the room" with them emotionally. If you have not separated sufficiently from your family of origin, your parents are right there with you emotionally, often hindering you from cleaving to your spouse and becoming one. If you have unhealed pain or unresolved issues involving your parents, there is a good chance this present and continuing conflict is keeping you from enjoying the depth of intimacy God has intended for you and your family.

Your parents' unhealthy intrusion into your life may take one of a number of different forms. We have identified four significant unresolved issues that seem to create the majority of the parental baggage couples bring into their marriages: unfulfilled expectations, unsure identity, unhealthy thinking, and unhealed emotions.

## UNFULFILLED EXPECTATIONS

As children, we are dependent on our parents and other adults for almost everything. It is natural for us to expect our parents to be there to meet our physical and emotional needs. Yet as we grow to adulthood and marry, God desires that we redirect our expectations to him and trust that he will meet them in his way and time. And he meets a measure of those needs through our spouses. But if you have not left father and mother by transferring your expectations from them to God and your spouse, intimacy in your relationship will be seriously hindered.

For Doug and Ruth, failing to resolve unfulfilled expectations had negatively affected their marriage and Doug's ministry. Doug had been a pastor for over twenty years, and his life was tangled into quite a knot. He was a workaholic, and he was constantly in trouble with Ruth for spending too much time at the church. Furthermore, he had upset the church board by accepting outside speaking engagements and moneymaking ventures that conflicted with his church responsibilities. Elders and denominational leaders had been forced to put Doug on a short leash by closely regulating the amount of time he was away.

Doug was also in his fourth year of financial counseling due to a deep crater of debt. He had taken Ruth on trips and bought her things they could not afford. He had "maxed out" credit cards with bills he could not pay. Doug was overextended in every area of his life, and their marriage was on the brink of collapse.

Doug and Ruth attended one of our marriage retreats a few years ago. We often have couples fill out a family-information questionnaire before we talk to them, so Doug and Ruth brought their forms with them. One of the questions on the sheet was, "How did your father praise you?" We noticed that Ruth had left this question blank.

"Looks as if you really missed your dad's praise, is that right?" I asked.

Tears welled up in her eyes. "Yes, and it hurts me deeply because Daddy is the most important man in my life."

How would you feel if you were Doug? Ruth's revealing statement provided a clear view to a root issue in their marriage problems. Doug had spent the last twenty years trying to overtake Ruth's father for first place in her heart. Responding to unmet needs for approval in his own life, Doug had worked long hours to show that he could care for his wife. He had sought outside speaking engagements and get-rich-quick schemes to earn extra money. He had spent everything he earned and more trying to please Ruth and gain her primary affection. But she still regarded her father as the most important man in her life.

Oneness in Doug and Ruth's marriage was being hindered as Ruth still turned to her father to fill her need for appreciation and approval instead of trusting God to work through her husband. Important times of mourning and comforting followed as God worked to deepen their sense of leaving and cleaving.

As we talked later, Doug mentioned that he and Ruth would be visiting her parents for a few days. I took him aside and challenged him with an assignment to help his wife take an additional step toward leaving her father. I suggested that, during the visit, he state to his in-laws in Ruth's hearing how happy he was that he was her husband and that she was his wife. He did not understand why I gave him the assignment, but he agreed to do it.

The next time Doug and I got together, he was beaming as he shared with me what happened. At the close of the visit with Ruth's parents, Doug and Ruth were ready to walk out the door. The luggage was packed in the trunk of the car, and the children were in the backseat. Doug stood beside Ruth, wrapped his arm around her shoulders, and faced her parents. "You know, Mom and Dad, I don't think I've ever told you this before, but you have a very, very special daughter. And I'm thrilled that she's *my* wife! I just want you to know that. Bye."

As Doug turned to walk out the door, Ruth looked at her father and then back at her husband. Then she broke into tears—happy tears, she later shared with us. Ruth was able to take a giant step toward leaving her parents when Doug's simple, loving statement met a significant need for acceptance and approval in her life. Once in the car, the couple took a giant step toward cleaving and becoming one. "As we drove away, Ruth slid over beside me and put her arm around me," Doug related. "And she hadn't done that in over ten years."

Intimacy is deepened when we redirect our expectations from our parents to God, trusting him to meet our needs in part through our spouses. Leaving your father and mother in this way may be a scary thing for you. You likely have come to expect certain things emotionally from Mom, Dad, and other adult caregivers in your life. Redirecting these expectations to God, who is

*INTIMACY is deepened when we redirect our expectations from our parents to God, trusting him to meet our needs in part through our spouses.*

free to involve your spouse in meeting them, is a critical part of leaving your father and mother.

The key is to look to God for needs, not to your spouse. We are to cast all our anxiety on the Lord because he cares for us (see 1 Peter 5:7). Directing your expectations toward your spouse leads to selfish "taking," which never satisfies. Trusting God's promise to meet all your needs will deepen your faith and free you to cleave to your partner. As you trust God to meet your needs, your fears will subside.

## UNCERTAIN IDENTITY

Marty and Della were married in the spring, and their new life together was like heaven on earth. The magic of their two-week honeymoon seemed to last for months. But the honeymoon ended abruptly in the fall, when Della brought up a topic they had never talked about before.

"You're going to love Christmas at my parents' place," she said as the two of them puttered in the garage one Saturday morning. "It's wild and crazy and loud, but it's wonderful."

Marty stopped sweeping up sawdust and turned to his wife, who was putting away tools on the workbench. "Christmas at your parents' house?" he said, eyes narrowing beneath a furrowed brow.

"Of course," Della chirped. "I have always been home for Christmas with my parents, three brothers, two sisters, and their families. It's barely October, and I'm already excited about it."

Marty leaned the push broom against the wall and stepped toward his wife. "But, sweetheart, this is our first Christmas together as husband and wife. I want us to spend a quiet, relaxed day together in our own home, just the two of us. Can't we see your family on Christmas Eve or the day after Christmas?"

"And miss being there for the best day of the year?" Della exclaimed in disbelief. "Marty, you have to be kidding. I can't miss out on Dad's famous eggnog and Mom's ham dinner with au gratin potatoes."

"We could spend the morning here together and go over for dinner later," Marty suggested. "I'll fix my famous veggie and cheese omelet and serve you breakfast in bed."

Della shook her head. "I have to be at Mom and Dad's early to see the nieces and nephews tear open their gifts together. Then we all have cinnamon rolls and play with their new toys. That's the way we've always had Christmas."

"But we could—"

"Marty, I *have* to be with my family on Christmas Day," Della interrupted. "It just wouldn't be Christmas for me."

Marty's shoulders slumped. "What about Christmas for *me?*" he whined. "Doesn't my vote count for anything?"

"We're alone together most of the time," Della countered, "and I enjoy our quiet, relaxing days together too." Then her hands went to her hips in a mock pose of defiance as she added, "Just as long as one of them is not Christmas."

Marty scowled. "Well, I hope you have a good time, Della, because I'm spending at least part of Christmas Day in my own home." Then he stormed out of the garage.

Why were Marty and Della unable to come to a compromise? The issue has less to do with Christmas celebration styles than with failing to leave father and mother. We're not saying that a couple cannot celebrate holidays with their parents. But each husband and wife must determine the distinctiveness of their own family and fit their respective families of origin into that picture instead of the other way around. This includes not only how you celebrate holidays but also a myriad of tasks and responsibilities for which you must decide how you two will operate.

*$\mathcal{E}$ACH husband and wife must determine the distinctiveness of their own family and fit their respective families of origin into that picture instead of the other way around.*

Growing up with your parents, you may have naturally assumed that their way of doing things was the way things ought to be done. Your parents' personalities, preferences, convictions, and gender roles shaped your own in everything from what meals are served on certain days, to who mows the grass, to where you go on vacation, to how you deal with conflict. You brought these expectations, preferences, and habits into your marriage, and your spouse brought his or her own unique set. But now you must determine under God your own pattern for living together—even if it ends up being a healthy composite of what you each brought into your relationship. Failing to leave father and mother in these areas can result in some painful aloneness in your marriage.

For Teresa and me, this journey was marked by many hard-fought battles. For example, we clashed over who should take out the trash in our home. Teresa's daddy did it in her family, but my dad delegated that job, so our expectations were different. When conflicts occurred in my family of origin, you were to shut up and deal with it. After all, you don't talk back to a marine drill sergeant. In Teresa's family no one expressed open conflict. Her mom would go to another room and cry, and her dad would bark and say hurtful things. Teresa didn't learn how to express her hurt or how to share the hurt, so it came out in anger. I experienced many painful years of Teresa's shouting at me in anger, and she had to deal with the aggravation of me clamming up when we had a problem.

If skirmishes like these sound familiar, it is because they are common to most marriages. We often tend to impose expectations from our families of origin on our own family life. The following steps will help you leave father and mother in this area by guiding you to determine the distinctives of your own home.

1. **Decide what items to keep.** Talk together to identify which traits and traditions from your families of origin you wish to maintain in your own marriage and family. This will allow you to express what was important and meaningful to you growing up.

Celebrate together certain elements of tradition, routine, or style you think are worth preserving in your own family.

**2. Determine why you want to keep them.** Vulnerably share with each other why you wish to preserve certain distinctives from your family of origin. These motives may be healthy or unhealthy. For example, perpetuating a certain tradition because it is meaningful to you and your family is healthy, but perpetuating a tradition out of fear of family disapproval is unhealthy. Don't be afraid to say something like, "A big part of why I want to spend Christmas with my family is because Dad will be angry with me if I don't."

**3. Trust God to help you create something uniquely yours.** Each of you likely brought into your first home together a collection of hand-me-down furniture, dishes, and knickknacks from your parents' homes. You sorted through what you had, bought a few new pieces, and blended it all to create your own unique living area. Similarly, as you sort through your preferences and expectations, you need to arrive at a healthy compromise that works for both of you. Trust God's direction as you do this. He knows each of you and your children as no one else does, and you can count on him to guide you into a plan that will allow for greater intimacy in your relationship.

## Unhealthy Thinking

Carol surveyed her garden of azaleas. She and her husband, Greg, had recently moved into a new home, and Carol had already begun to beautify the yard by planting her favorite flowers.

Proud of what she had done, she motioned Greg over from mowing the grass. "How does it look?" she asked eagerly.

"Yeah, it looks fine," Greg replied.

"Just 'fine'?" Carol probed. "Don't you like it?"

"It's not the flowers," Greg said. "I'm just wondering if there is enough greenery there to make the flowers stand out."

Carol dropped her head and released a sigh of disappointment tinged with irritation. Then she slowly removed her gardening gloves. "There's just no way I can please you, is there?" she said, heading into the house.

Greg followed her in. "Carol, what I said had nothing to do with how I see you," he protested. "I was simply sharing my opinion on the garden. That's what you asked for, isn't it? For goodness sakes, don't take everything so personally."

By the time Greg and Carol participated in one of our advanced training conferences, many scenes like this had played out over the years of their marriage. Carol admitted that any hint of criticism or disapproval by Greg was a crushing blow to her personally. "What makes it so bad," Carol related to us, "is that it often ruins a perfectly wonderful day or evening together. Even after Greg explains that he didn't mean to hurt me, the episode shuts me down emotionally and I feel so removed from him. What can we do?"

Carol grew up with an overly critical father, and his disapproval replays in her emotions whenever she senses that Greg is not pleased with her in some way. It is as if Carol's father is right there in the room with them, criticizing her through Greg. So an innocent question like "Is there enough greenery in the flower bed?" comes through as her father saying, "Why can't you do anything right?"

Carol's problem is not uncommon. Perhaps you have struggled with unhealthy thinking. Even though you have left your father and mother physically, their negative attitudes and messages are still with you, blocking your oneness with your spouse. You may have grown up feeling that you were unacceptable or unlovable or unworthy. You may have felt a lack of approval or appreciation. Such unhealthy messages may have come from your parents, other relatives, teachers, coaches, schoolmates, or other sources. But when they surface in your marriage, they only serve to keep you from the intimacy you seek with your spouse.

In order to counter this negative programming from the past, you must leave your unhealthy thinking about yourself and replace it with the truth. You need to adopt God's correct view of you and realize that he desires to involve your spouse in affirming your true value and significance. You need to leave your unhealthy thinking and cleave to your spouse, trusting God to affirm his truth through him or her.

This is what we shared with Carol. She agreed, saying she desperately wanted to be free of the old programming that had driven a painful wedge between her and Greg. "But," she objected, almost in tears, "I just can't keep from emotionally shutting down when I sense my father's disapproval."

We suggested an exercise to help Carol leave the old programming and cleave to the truth about herself as shared by Greg. Whenever she sensed her father's disapproval in her relationship with Greg, Carol was to tell Greg about it and declare it to be a lie. Then Greg was to counter that lie with the truth in the form of positive affirmation. Specifically, we suggested that Carol allow Greg to embrace her and whisper in her ear, "I love you for being you, and I always will." The couple agreed to try the exercise.

*A*LONENESS *is removed and oneness is deepened when you and your spouse leave the lies of unhealthy thinking and help each other embrace the truth about yourselves.*

A few months later, Carol reported back to us. "I can't believe it. The simple exercise of Greg's holding me close and whispering those affirming words to me has turned things around. It's as if I'm being reprogrammed. I am becoming free from the past, and Greg and I are closer than ever before."

Aloneness is removed and oneness is deepened when you and your spouse leave the lies of unhealthy thinking and help each other embrace the truth about yourselves.

## UNHEALED EMOTIONS
Inevitably all of us have experienced the pain of certain unmet needs. We grew up as imperfect persons in the care of imperfect

persons, so disappointments, rejections, and unmet needs were inevitable. The issue is not whether you experienced such pain but whether you have found healing and freedom from the pain. Unless you are able to leave those childhood hurts behind, they will likely hinder intimacy in your marriage.

Teresa shares how not leaving a childhood hurt had hindered intimacy in our marriage: "David and I had just concluded a pastors' conference in Atlanta. We were on a tight schedule for our flight home, but we were also hungry. So David dropped me off at the terminal while he returned the rental car. He pulled some money out of his pocket—a few ones and a fifty-dollar bill—and handed it to me. After checking our bags at the curb and tipping the skycap, I went to the restaurant and ordered our lunch.

"When we finished our lunch, David asked me for the fifty dollars so he could pay the bill. But when I reached into my pocket, the money was gone. Apparently I had dropped the large bill when I pulled the money out of my pocket to tip the skycap. When I realized the money was gone, my fifty-dollar mistake ballooned into a five-thousand-dollar tragedy in my mind. I began tearing myself down and berating myself, saying something like, 'I am so stupid. I am so dumb. I can't believe I lost fifty dollars.' "

Teresa's self-condemning response to this incident only made her disappointment worse. Even though I repeatedly stated to her that I was not upset at her losing the fifty dollars, it seemed to make little difference. She was angry with herself, and she wasn't about to let herself off the hook. This had become a pattern in Teresa's life, fueling a negative emotional reaction that in turn seemed to lock me out of her life.

As I persisted with sympathetic and reassuring words, it seemed to calm her down. As she allowed herself to receive my comfort, she found freedom to explore a childhood issue that had contributed to her tendency toward self-condemnation. It also prompted a childhood memory that she related to me.

"As I was growing up, you know that our family lived on very little. Money was a big deal in our home because there usually wasn't enough to go around. I had considerable anxiety over money as a child, but one particular incident stood out.

"One day I was sent to the grocery story to get a few things for a Girl Scout event of mine, but on the way I lost the money. It was a childish mistake, and I felt terrible. I returned home and shared what had happened, deeply needing Mom's acceptance and support. Instead, I was scolded severely and ordered back outside to look for the money alone.

"This unhealed hurt was suddenly exposed when I discovered that the fifty-dollar bill was gone. My mind was filled with self-condemning thoughts—'It's all my fault. I never do anything right.' My heart was flooded with a helpless sense of aloneness, reminding me of how much of my childhood I spent alone. The lost fifty-dollar bill had touched a wound that was not just from the one-time event of looking for the Girl Scout money, but from a pattern of often struggling alone."

Teresa needed my acceptance at that point, and I freely gave it. But even as I was trying to offer reassuring words, she was hearing the disapproving words of her mother right there in the airport. We could not really cleave as a couple at this point until Teresa could somehow leave this unhealed wound from her past.

There wasn't anything for me to confess since I had not contributed to Teresa's pain in this case. But God was pleased to involve me in ministering his comfort to her in order to see a depth of freedom that had been needed for decades. Comfort is what frees us from the unhealed hurts of the past. As Teresa mourned the pain of her wounded emotions, I was able to mourn with her (see Matthew 5:4 and Romans 12:15), and she was blessed by God's comforting words through me.

I said something like, "Teresa, it deeply saddens me to think of you as a young girl unintentionally losing money and being scolded for it, feeling so condemned. It also hurts me that you were so often alone. You needed someone's care and love, and yet it often wasn't there for you. I'm very sorry you hurt like that because I love you. It saddens me to think of you hurting."

God was faithful that day to honor his Word. The God of all comfort ministered an added dimension of healing to Teresa's pain, and we experienced a deeper level of oneness. Freedom from years of self-condemning thoughts was underway as Teresa began to sense a deepened dimension of worth in the eyes of her heavenly Father.

About a month later, Teresa was in another airport on her way to speak at a women's conference. Standing alone in front of a security checkpoint, she looked down to find a fifty-dollar bill lying at her feet. There was no one else around, so she picked up the money and—encouraged by the security guard—put it in her pocket. We believe God dropped that bill there just to express to Teresa how much he accepts her, approves of her, and is attentive to her needs.

Experiencing God's Word in our marriage does work. The biblical principle to leave father and mother and cleave to our spouse is as relevant today as it was when God issued it to Adam and Eve. Experiencing the principle of leaving frees us to enjoy the cleaving of intimacy. As we pass that legacy on to our children and grandchildren, God is blessed by the loving community we are perpetuating.

But leaving our father and mother is more than leaving unfulfilled expectations, uncertain identity, unhealthy thinking, and unhealed emotions. In the next chapter we will explore how leaving our father and mother also frees us to honor our father and mother.

# CHAPTER 12

# Leaving to Honor Father and Mother

L eaving your father and mother to cleave to your spouse isn't like leaving Egypt for the Promised Land. Your parents are not a plague to be avoided. Rather they are special people to be honored. The leaving and cleaving process simply lays the proper foundation for a healthy, ongoing relationship with your parents. In reality, if you fail to develop and maintain a healthy adult relationship with your parents, your marriage relationship may suffer for it. But when you leave father and mother as the Bible directs, you are free to deepen your oneness as husband and wife. And God receives the community of love he is looking for in your marriage.

The leaving and cleaving process initiates a God-ordained chain reaction of blessing. Leaving parents frees you to experience deeper intimacy in marriage and enables you to impart your lives more effectively to your children and others. Leaving your father and mother also frees you to honor your parents according to Ephesians 6:2-3: " 'Honor your father and mother'—which is the first commandment with a promise—'that it may go well with you and that you may enjoy long life on the earth' " (NIV). And leaving your father and

*IF you fail to develop and maintain a healthy adult relationship with your parents, your marriage relationship may suffer for it.*

mother frees you to extend God's living legacy through your family to future generations.

Ephesians 6:2-3 promises that, as we honor our parents, we will enjoy a good and long life. Part of that good life, no doubt, is the peace and fulfillment of deepened marital oneness, manifesting the living legacy of God's community. But it all begins with honoring father and mother.

## IN HONOR OF DAD AND MOM

Honoring parents means showing respect, holding them in high esteem, and exalting them as valued persons. Lee, a minister friend, recently indicated to me that his father did not deserve any respect *as a person* because of the way he had treated Lee as a child. But Lee said he would show respect to him *as a father,* since the man occupied that role. So Lee did invite his dad over for family gatherings, gave him cards and gifts on holidays, and spoke *to* him and *about* him to others "respectfully."

Lee had shared with me vulnerably about his difficult childhood and struggles with his father. I asked him, "When you invite your father over or give him gifts, do you do it with a grateful heart?"

He pondered the question for a moment, then said, "Honestly, I don't have a lot of gratefulness in my heart toward my father."

"Not even for the good things he provided for you as a child?" I asked.

"I suppose he has done some good things for me," he responded, "but those memories rarely come to mind."

Why was Lee ungrateful for the good in his father and unable to truly honor him as a person? Are we to honor our parents only if they have been model parents? Every relationship includes positive and negative qualities. Everyone has strengths and weaknesses. There is no such thing as a perfect person or a perfect parent. But if we have unresolved issues with our parents, those issues will hinder us from being as grateful as God would want us to be for our parents' positive traits. And a lack of gratefulness will keep us from truly honoring them.

I probed Lee further. "Have you fully forgiven your father for how he treated you as a child?"

"I'm not sure I have *fully* forgiven him," he said slowly. "Maybe that's why I don't feel very grateful toward him."

Lee was getting the point, so I went on. "Have you asked your father to forgive you for *your* failures or anything *you* may have said or done that needs to be confessed?"

I could tell this topic made Lee uncomfortable. "David, it's hard enough to think that it's possible that I may not have fully forgiven my father for how he treated me, let alone apologize to him for something I might have done."

I understood Lee's struggle. I had personally struggled with similar feelings toward my father. But we must seek the forgiveness of others for the hurts we have caused them. And I believe as we seek forgiveness, it helps release us from offenses we feel they have committed against us. It is nearly impossible to forgive someone without a contrite heart that first deals with our own faults.

Jesus said, "For in the way you judge, you will be judged; and by your standard of measure, it will be measured to you" (Matt. 7:2). This is certainly true about forgiveness. We are to forgive others just as God has forgiven us (see Ephesians 4:32). Jesus told his disciples, "But when you are praying, first forgive anyone you are holding a grudge against, so that your Father in heaven will forgive your sins, too" (Mark 11:25, NLT).

Forgiving others, no matter how badly they have hurt us, is a direct command from God. And he never tells us to do something without also empowering us to obey the command. Just as he provides the healing power of comfort for your hurts, he will also provide the liberating power of forgiveness toward those who hurt you, including your parents.

## THE HEALING POWER OF FORGIVENESS

In one sense, forgiveness completes the emotional healing process. Forgiveness is a beautiful gift from the God who has our best interests at heart. To refuse God's gift is to remain in bondage to the pain of the past. God wants us to forgive so we can put away our anger and experience the full healing that comes from his comfort.

Soon after I became a Christian, I felt deep conviction over the disrespect and rebellion I had exhibited toward my parents. My subsequent brokenness and tear-filled confession had gone a long way toward healing our relationship. I was in the process of forgiving my father and mother so I could cleave more intimately to my wife. But like my friend Lee, I still related to my father more out of cordial concern than the honoring love needed to break down the barriers between us as father and son.

Early in my ministry to students I was often complimented for my sense of humor. I guess I came by it honestly, because my father had a wonderful sense of humor. He always made family trips fun and brought joy to the most boring situations. But I discounted compliments about my humor, saying things like, "Humor is unimportant to me because I want to be a serious student of the Word." In reality, my own unresolved issues with Dad hindered me from fully appreciating his strengths.

As the internal process of healing, forgiveness, and leaving-and-cleaving began for me, I was free to embrace and appreciate my father's contributions to my life, including his marvelous sense of humor. As I freely received this gift, God began to use it in my ministry. It was a significant step for me in learning to honor my father despite the pain we had experienced in our relationship.

Then I started writing notes of appreciation to Dad and Mom. On the occasion of one of their special wedding anniversaries, I wrote what our friend Dennis Rainey, director of FamilyLife Ministry, calls a "tribute" to Mom and Dad. Whenever we got together with my parents, I sought to share memories of special blessings from our relationship. I looked for ways to praise my parents privately and publicly. I took the initiative to communicate my care, concern, and love for them regularly. My parents were being honored, and God was being pleased.

Then came a challenge I did not expect. God seemed to say, "Why not tell your dad about the kind of relationship you still want to enjoy with him?"

I responded, "God, you must be kidding. I'm a grown man. I have a wife, three kids, an intimate relationship with you, and a growing ministry. Why do I need a deeper relationship with Dad at this point?"

God seemed to answer my question with a question: "What hinders you from experiencing Ephesians 4:15—'speaking the truth in love' (NIV)—with your dad?"

The answer was immediately apparent to me: fear. I was still afraid Dad would reject me. God seemed to say, "David, if you let me, I will drive out your fear with my perfect love."

After months of arguing with God, praying, and seeking counsel from Teresa and others, D day finally arrived. Blessed by Teresa's ministry of comfort, I was confident that, as I faced my fear, the truth would come out in love as I became vulnerable to Dad with humility and gentleness. Regardless of the outcome, I knew that God and Teresa were there for me; even if I experienced additional hurt, God's comfort from himself and through Teresa would be there for me.

A holiday family gathering brought Dad and me together. We were in my parents' backyard discussing the latest urban encroachments on the serenity of their lovely home. Developers were busy at work across Dad's back fence, daily covering his trees and shrubs with dust and disturbing his dog.

*G*OD *wants us to forgive so we can put away our anger and experience the full healing that comes from his comfort.*

In what must have sounded like the most awkward conversation transition of all time, I blurted out, "Dad, I've been thinking. Now that I have my own kids, I realize that I haven't been as close to you as I would like, and I'm looking forward to changing that." Then I hugged him and hurried into the house before he could say anything. The truth had been spoken in love, I had faced a measure of my fear, and I sensed God's pleasure.

Dad did not respond to my comment that day or for the next several months, even though we were in contact frequently. Then another holiday brought us together again. We were alone in the kitchen putting our plates into the dishwasher. This time it was Dad who spoke first, and from his first word I knew something special was about to happen.

He began by speaking my name in a calm, gentle voice: "David." That was very significant to me. For most of my life Dad called me Son. As a military man, he addressed people by their rank or title. My rank was "Son," just like that of my younger brother—which caused confusion in our family at times. But at the sound of my father's voice speaking my name, tears immediately came to my eyes.

Then I heard a tough drill sergeant's version of a contrite confession: "David, I've been thinking. I was rough as a cob on you growing up. But you turned out all right." Then, to top it off, he hugged me!

After our awkward embrace, the tender interlude was over. But our relationship had taken a giant step forward. From that day on, we began to develop common interests. Our conversations grew deeper and more personal. Contacting Dad and spending time with him became a pleasure for me, not a duty. We even laughed together about how he bounced quarters off my sheets during bed inspections. A genuine friendship developed between us. A father was honored, and a son was blessed.

## RESOLVING PARENTAL ISSUES AND DEEPENING MARITAL INTIMACY: AN EXERCISE

The next few pages offer practical steps for dealing with any unresolved issues with your parents. Then you will find an exercise to deepen and enrich your marriage relationship. We believe you will find that the more God frees you to leave your father and mother by dealing with unresolved issues, the more you will be free to cleave to your spouse.

Each of you will need to complete the following exercise. You may want to do it on blank sheets of paper, or you may photocopy these pages for your use. Then take turns sharing your responses with each other.

**1. Confess.** As you reflect on your growing-up years and adult life, allow God to bring to your heart ways in which you may have hurt your parents or other caregivers through rebellion, disrespect, insensitivity, rejection, or ungratefulness. Pray: *Heavenly Father, bring to my mind areas for which I need to confess and seek forgiveness.*

My father

_____

My mother

_____

Other caregivers

_____

Acknowledge your responsibility to God, experience his sorrow, then rejoice gratefully in his promised forgiveness (see 1 John 1:9). Describe your plans to experience James 5:16, "Confess your sins to one another," with each parent or other caregiver. (For example, will you make a personal visit or call on the phone or write a letter?)

_____

_____

_____

_____

**2. Leave**. We must no longer look to our family of origin to meet needs God desires to meet through our spouse. Review the key intimacy needs discussed in chapter 5: comfort, attention, acceptance, appreciation, support, encouragement, affection, respect, security, and approval. Consider ways you may still be looking to parents to meet these needs. Write your reflections below.

I still may be inappropriately seeking _____ from Dad.
I still may be inappropriately seeking _____ from Mom.
I still may be inappropriately seeking _____ from
_____.

After sharing this information with your husband or wife, pray together. Ask God to bless you abundantly in these areas through your spouse.

**3. Comfort**. Reflect again on the key needs discussed in chapter 5, giving particular attention to those needs that, to a significant degree, went unmet during your growing-up years. Note the ways you may have been hurt as a result. Be as specific as possible, even citing specific incidents that caused you pain.

I believe I missed/needed more _____ from my father. It hurt me that _____

_____

I believe I missed/needed more _____ from my mother. It hurt me that _____

_____

I believe I missed/needed more _____ from _____. It hurt
me that _____

_____

Once you have completed your reflections, share them with your
spouse. Mourn your loss and pain together, then share and
receive God's comfort. Listen intently as your partner shares
personal reflections, seeking to capture the Father's heart of
compassion for him or her. How did God feel when your spouse
experienced that pain? Imagine Jesus being moved with
compassion, wrapping his arms around your husband or wife
and hurting with him or her.

Participate in God's compassionate care. Resist the temptation to
counsel, correct, instruct, or fix the problem. Simply be God's channel
of his comfort.

**4. Forgive.** Forgiveness is an issue of stewardship. We choose to
share with others the unmerited gift of God's forgiveness as we have
received it from him. In reality, the forgiveness we share is not really
ours; it is his. Will you share with your parents some of the
forgiveness God has shared with you? It may help to briefly journal
below your prayerful choice to forgive.

Heavenly Father, I choose to forgive _____
concerning _____.
Thank you, Father, for forgiving me and prompting me to forgive
others.

**5. Honor.** Having initiated God's healing in your relationships
by confessing, leaving, comforting, and forgiving, you are now
more free to honor your parents with a grateful heart. Reflect on
the character strengths and qualities you appreciate in your
parents.

I appreciate my father for _____.
I appreciate my mother for _____.
I appreciate _____ for _____.

List four ways you can share your insights with them:

_____

_____

_____

_____


AN EXERCISE IN DEEPENED ONENESS

Unhealed pain and an unforgiving heart can keep you from experiencing the oneness God desires in your marriage. As your wounded heart is comforted and you are empowered to forgive your parents, you will experience additional freedom to deepen oneness with your spouse. Deepening your relationship with your spouse is an ongoing, daily process. Painful childhood memories may surface over time, and they will require you to mourn with and comfort each other. God has given you the privilege to comfort your spouse's hurt and then move in to meet his or her needs on a consistent basis. As hurts are healed and needs are met, you will experience deepened oneness.

Each of you will need to complete the following exercise. You may want to do it on blank sheets of paper, or you may photocopy these pages for your use. Then take turns sharing your responses with each other.

**1. Meet your spouse's needs**. Consider needs that were abundantly met in your spouse by parents and other caregivers during his or her growing-up years (circle two or three):

| | |
|---|---|
| Comfort | Encouragement |
| Attention | Affection |
| Acceptance | Respect |
| Appreciation | Security |
| Support | Approval |

Since God desires to bless your spouse primarily through you instead of through his or her parents, oneness in your marriage will be enriched as you develop increased sensitivity to meeting the needs you circled.

Now consider needs that were unmet in some significant way during your spouse's growing-up years (circle two or three):

| | |
|---|---|
| Comfort | Encouragement |
| Attention | Affection |
| Acceptance | Respect |
| Appreciation | Security |
| Support | Approval |

Be aware that your spouse will benefit from God's love through you as you are diligent to meet the needs you circled.

**2. Think of your spouse first**. Adopting Christ's unselfish attitude is critical to expressing love, cleaving to one another, and building oneness in your marriage. Review the following passage, noting Christ's example of giving himself for us. Then express in the spaces below ways you are challenged to sacrifice in order to encourage oneness with your spouse.

> "Have this attitude in yourselves which was also in Christ Jesus, who, although He existed in the form of God, did not regard equality with God a thing to be grasped, but emptied Himself, taking the form of a bond-servant, and being made in the likeness of men. And being found in appearance as a man, He humbled Himself by becoming obedient to the point of death, even death on a cross." (Phil. 2:5-8)

In order to better express Christ's love to my spouse . . .

I need to consider giving up _____

I need to give priority to _____

I need to avoid _____

**3. Take the initiative**. A significant aspect of God's love for us is demonstrated in his initiative. He sent his Son to redeem us while we were yet sinners (see Romans 5:8). Similarly, his love will be powerfully demonstrated through you to your spouse when you take the initiative to offer loving words and deeds. This may include such things as writing and sending notes, phone calls in the middle of the day, surprise dates, volunteering to help with projects, and purchasing gifts. Write your plans by answering this question:

What steps of loving initiative can I take to better express unselfish love to my spouse today?

_____

_____

_____

Close this exercise by asking God to help you deepen your relationship with your spouse through these steps.

# CHAPTER 13

# Keeping Marriage Alive and Well

I love Shawn and all, but . . ." Marla paused, searching for the right words. Shawn shifted in his chair, nervously anticipating what his wife was about to share. The couple had come to us for help with a marriage problem.

Marla continued, "It's just that our marriage has sort of leveled off. We don't talk a lot anymore. The real closeness is gone. Sex isn't what it used to be and—"

"What sex?" Shawn snorted derisively.

"Yes, well, I know we don't do it much anymore," Marla replied.

Shawn leaned forward. "Did you hear that: 'do it'? That's all it means to her anymore. Sex is something she has to do once in a while, like cleaning the toilets. I think if we never had sex again, Marla would be perfectly happy!"

Marla quickly countered, "And if Shawn never took me on another romantic night out like he did when we were dating, *he'd* be perfectly happy!"

This couple was obviously lacking in the intimacy department. Things had been changing in their relationship. Marla had quit her job to care for their two children, and Shawn was working longer hours. Their frantic weekly schedule had them on the go, with little time for just the two of them. The romance and sexual magic of their marriage had cooled. Shawn and Marla loved each other, but they didn't know how to keep their relationship growing and thriving. After ten years together, they needed a fresh direction for their marriage.

Oneness in marriage is not automatic. Keeping the intimacy in marriage alive and vibrant requires thoughtful care, or love will grow cold. Intimacy must be purposely maintained and deepened on three vital fronts: emotional, physical, and spiritual. We refer to this three-pronged emphasis as becoming more intimate friends, lovers, and saints.

## FRIENDS: KEEPING YOUR EMOTIONAL RELATIONSHIP ALIVE AND WELL

Friendship in marriage needs to be cultivated on a regular basis. Here are four important ways to revitalize your friendship:

1. **Make time for each other.** Friends set apart time to be together, and a husband and wife need to cultivate their friendship by planning time for togetherness. Making time for your spouse signals that he or she is very special to you. Set aside some time each day to talk together, debrief about your day, communicate on calendar items, discuss current events, as well as share dreams and concerns. Take turns choosing fun things to do together—a sport, a hobby, cultural events, concerts, home-improvement tasks, or a continuing education class. Give your spouse time priority when he or she needs help with a two-person project. Marital friendship will likely *include* romance and sex, but if the only quality time you spend together is for lovemaking, your friendship will lack richness and depth.

2. **Heal hurts and meet needs.** Even the best of friends hurt each other occasionally. Every marriage has its share of hurtful words, misunderstandings, dashed expectations, and unmet needs. But enduring friends care enough to resolve hurts and take pains to meet each other's needs. This is an ongoing process that requires attention and effort. It takes time to learn what your spouse needs

and discern the best ways to meet those needs. But friendship is deepened as your spouse senses your commitment to meet his or her needs and deal with the inevitable hurts.

**3. Practice emotional responding.** Friends not only communicate on an intellectual level; they also communicate on an emotional level. Asking, "What do you think?" is pretty natural, but asking "What are you feeling?" is more of a learned skill. Friendship in marriage is enriched as you learn to respond to each other emotionally as well as intellectually. Productive emotional responding sounds something like this: "I can see that you're hurting; please tell me how you feel"; "I want to understand how I have hurt you and make it right"; "Your comment tapped into some painful emotions I would like to share with you."

**4. Speak the truth in love.** Close friends should be truthful with each other, but truth must be shared in love or it will cause further hurt instead of facilitate healing. Before you share something your spouse needs to hear, like how he or she may have hurt you, make sure your comment is motivated by love. Think about how you would like to be told about a shortcoming. Would you rather hear "I can't believe how thoughtless and insensitive you were!" or "I know you didn't mean to and you might not have even noticed, but I felt a lack of respect when . . ."? Be sensitive and share from a loving heart. Avoid sharing anything about how your spouse may have hurt you until you are able to share your hurt in a loving way.

## LOVERS: KEEPING YOUR PHYSICAL RELATIONSHIP ALIVE AND WELL

Good sex doesn't lead to oneness; oneness leads to good sex. Coming together physically deepens intimacy in marriage only when you are already in the process of coming together emotionally and spiritually. Sex is not primarily something you *do* or something you *have;* sex is something you share.

If you consider sex something you *do,* you will tend to evaluate it like other things you do: how often you should do it, how long since you've done it, how adept you are at doing it, or how you can get better at doing it. Treating sex like other physical activities such as golf or tennis does not promote intimacy.

*S*EX *is not primarily something you do or something you have; sex is something you share.*

If you consider sex something you *have,* you will tend to evaluate it like other possessions. You may regard it as something useful in negotiating, trading, bargaining, or manipulation. For example, a spouse might say, "If you clean the garage today, I will initiate sex tonight" or "You let me watch the game tonight, so I owe you a passionate interlude."

God did not design sexual intimacy to be reduced to numbers or negotiation. When sex centers on sharing and affirming each other's presence, both partners will sense that they are cherished and valued as persons, not just sexual partners. Sex is one very special way of being with your spouse. It contributes to true oneness only if it is enjoyed within the context of emotional and spiritual intimacy.

Here are a few suggestions for enhancing physical intimacy:

**1. Keep dating.** Take turns asking each other out and preparing special times together. Sit down with your calendars frequently, and block out time for romantic getaways without the children. Keep alive the romantic little things you enjoyed during your courtship days: visiting a special restaurant, listening to "our song," buying a favorite cologne, or taking romantic walks.

**2. Keep the romance alive.** Enhance the physical dimension of sex with love notes, a secret wink, or a special gift. Consider the impact of calling in the middle of the day to say, "Hi, honey. I was just thinking about you. I love you, and I'm looking forward to seeing you tonight."

**3. Add variety to your lovemaking.** Vary the atmosphere by changing locations or time of day. Use different types of lighting and candlelight. Surprise each other with new apparel. Experiment with new fragrances in the bedroom. Play your favorite music.

**4. Communicate openly.** Don't let your lovemaking be a guessing game, and don't assume that your spouse automatically knows what pleases you. Talk openly about what you desire sexually, and ask your partner to share what he or she desires. Verbalizing what you need does not discount the deed!

**5. Encourage your sexual desire.** Sex isn't all in your head, but a great deal of it *is!* Preparing for sex mentally can help put you in the right mood. Anticipating a romantic interlude and your spouse's participation will make coming together more meaningful and pleasurable. By preparing mentally through the day, your sexual desire will be aroused even before the two of you touch.

## SAINTS: KEEPING YOUR SPIRITUAL RELATIONSHIP ALIVE AND WELL

Physical and emotional intimacy are generally understood. But when it comes to nurturing spiritual intimacy, many couples wonder where to start. Is an intimate spiritual relationship based on attending the same church? holding identical beliefs? preferring the same translation of the Bible? We know what it means to pursue spiritual maturity as individuals. But what does it mean to pursue spiritual oneness as a couple? Here are some suggestions on where to begin:

**1. As individuals, commit to a new spiritual goal.** Getting closer to each other spiritually requires that you are getting closer to God individually. Continue to set and work toward spiritual goals for your personal life. As you each pursue your own relationship with

God, you will find greater spiritual intimacy with each other. You may want to establish a goal of reading through the entire New Testament in a year (one chapter a day will do it easily), memorizing a new Bible verse each week, establishing a daily devotional time, or applying yourself to an in-depth Bible study on a topic such as marriage, grace, glory, faith, or prayer.

**2. As a couple, begin by learning to pray together.** One of our recent surveys indicated that fewer than 15 percent of churchgoing couples pray together. You may be among the majority for a number of reasons: You are not sure what to say when you pray; you feel embarrassed or inhibited about praying aloud in front of your spouse; you can't pray as well as the minister; you might get corrected by your spouse.

We recommend that you begin by praying silently together. Spend a few minutes talking about the items you want to pray about: your own concerns, hopes, dreams, fears, problems with the children, finances, work, and other issues that you want to take to God. Then join hands, bow your heads, and pray silently for two or three minutes.

In time, as you become more comfortable in this setting, one of you may feel comfortable about praying a sentence or two aloud before you pray silently. As you spend these times together, you may sense a spiritual closeness you have never felt before. You may also find that a new emotional and physical closeness will follow.

A couple recently went through one of our intense four-day marriage retreats. They were deeply committed to their marriage and very much in love with each other. But they found that their hectic daily schedules sometimes left them feeling a little disconnected from each other and alone. The wife suggested that perhaps a short time in prayer together each morning before they went their separate ways could help. During the retreat they announced to the group that they had committed to a time of spiritual devotion each morning.

A few months later we heard back from the couple. They related that they began reading a short devotional together after breakfast each morning. Then they moved their chairs together and embraced as each said a short prayer. They each asked God's help in being the kind of spouse that met the other's needs. The husband told me, "David, you can't believe what a difference this has made for us. Since we started praying together, there has not been one day that we felt disconnected or distant from each other!"

Christ tells us, "Again I say to you, that if two of you agree on earth about anything that they may ask, it shall be done for them by My Father who is in heaven" (Matt. 18:19). Can you think of anything more powerful than two people, who in God's eyes are already one, praying together?

## THE FOUNDATION OF MARRIAGE

In Lewis Carroll's delightful story *Alice in Wonderland*, Alice encounters the grinning Cheshire Cat. Confronted with an assortment of paths leading off in all directions, Alice inquires of the cat, "Would you tell me, please, which way I ought to go from here?"

"That depends a good deal on where you want to get to," replies the Cat.

"I don't much know or care where," Alice says.

The Cheshire Cat insightfully responds, "Then it doesn't matter which way you go."

Alice's exchange with the Cheshire Cat reflects the dilemma in many marriages today. "If you don't know where you're going," as someone once said, "any road will get you there." In the ministry Teresa and I have to couples, we frequently hear complaints like "We don't seem to be getting anywhere!" and "I don't think we're accomplishing anything!" and "We just seem to be spinning our wheels!" A husband and wife generally arrive at this impasse because they have no idea what they are supposed to accomplish in their marriage, so they don't know whether they are succeeding or failing.

Wise Solomon said, "Where there is no vision, the people perish" (Prov. 29:18, KJV). The Hebrew word for *perish* in this verse is also translated "go unrestrained, each to his own way." This is a tragic but sadly fitting description of many marriages and families. Active and on the run, family members scurry through life at a helter-skelter pace, going their own way. They interface with each other but somehow fail to relate. Parents may talk to their children but often don't connect with them. Husbands and wives interact with each other but often feel relationally distant.

Marriages and families need a firm foundation and an encompassing framework for determining direction and making decisions. Amos 3:3 poses the question, "Can two people walk together without agreeing on the direction?" (NLT). It is essential in relationships that you agree about where you are going if you want to experience oneness. Marriage and family goal setting can help you, your spouse, and your children get on the same page.[2]

But for these goals to be meaningful in your marriage, they must rest on the one foundational goal or purpose of marriage. Remember: It's not what you get out of your marriage that matters most; it is what God gets out of your marriage. He desires something very special from your marriage: glory, honor, and pleasure. He is looking for a colleague in ministry to your spouse, a companion in ministry to him, a conduit of his glory and presence, and an ongoing community of intimate relationships. And when your goals are founded on giving God what he desires and deserves from your relationship, you and your family will be abundantly blessed.

This is part of the great mystery "into which angels long to look" (1 Pet. 1:12). Can you grasp it? God can receive from us something

[2]We have put together a detailed goal-setting tool in the Intimate Encounters workbook, which is referenced in appendix B of this book. This tool provides a step-by-step exercise for jointly establishing spiritual goals, marriage goals, family goals, household goals, financial goals, career/domestic goals, personal/social goals, and ministry goals.

that pleases him, and marriage is a divinely ordained relationship through which he desires to receive. The majestic, all-knowing, all-powerful God, who is complete in himself and needs nothing from us, can be blessed through your relationship with your spouse. Imagine a cluster of angels peering down from heaven at your relationship as husband and wife and saying, "Marriage and oneness are mysteries to us, but I think God is really going to be pleased with this one!"

We hope you have grown in awe and wonder that God desires to permeate your marriage and revel in the joy of your unique union. As your marriage expresses the intimacy of love, it pictures the Father's longing for his Son and his church. As your marriage portrays the oneness of caring involvement, it bears the image of the caring involvement between Father, Son, and Holy Spirit. As your marriage demonstrates the security and vulnerability of two people truly knowing and being known by one another, you give evidence and hope of God's "very good" in a lonely world that is not good.

*W*HEN your goals are founded on giving God what he desires and deserves from your relationship, you and your family will be abundantly blessed.

Such possibilities bring great depth of motivation to this life. For oneness in marriage returns to the Creator with the same strength as the eternal anthem of praise in the heavens: "Worthy is the Lamb . . . to receive power and riches and wisdom and might and honor and glory and blessing" (Rev. 5:12). It is for his pleasure that you and your spouse were created and called to oneness.

# APPENDIX A

# Intimacy Needs Assessment Inventory

INSTRUCTIONS
For each of the fifty statements below, enter the number that best represents your response to that statement. Then you may interpret your responses by completing the section "Identifying Your Top Needs."

| Strongly Disagree | Disagree | Neutral | Agree | Strongly Agree |
|---|---|---|---|---|
| -2 | -1 | 0 | +1 | +2 |

____ 1. It is important that people receive me for who I am, even if I'm a little "different."

__ 2. It is very important to me that my financial world be in order.

____ 3. I sometimes grow weary of doing my usual best.

____ 4. It is important to me that others seek my opinion.

____ 5. It is important that I receive frequent physical hugs, warm embraces, etc.

____ 6. I feel good when someone enters into my world and wants to know what I'm all about.

____ 7. It is important for me to know where I stand with those who are in authority over me.

____ 8. It is meaningful to me when someone notices that I need help and offers to get involved.

____ 9. I often feel overwhelmed. When this happens, I need someone to come alongside me and lighten my load.

____10. I feel blessed when someone notices and shows concern for how I'm doing emotionally.

____11. I like to know if what I do is of value to others.

____12. Generally speaking, I don't like a lot of solitude.

____13. It means a lot to me when a loved one says, "I love you."

____14. I resist being seen only as a part of a large group. Being recognized as an individual is important to me.

\_\_\_15. I feel blessed when someone calls just to hear me out and encourages me.

\_\_\_16. It is important to me that people acknowledge not only what I do but also who I am.

\_\_\_17. I feel best when my world is orderly and somewhat predictable.

\_\_\_18. I am pleased when people acknowledge my work on a project and express gratitude.

\_\_\_19. I especially enjoy completing a task when I am surrounded by others who like being with me.

\_\_\_20. I feel good when others notice my strengths and gifts.

\_\_\_21. I sometimes feel overwhelmed and discouraged.

\_\_\_22. I want to be treated with kindness and equality by all, regardless of my race, gender, looks, and status.

\_\_\_23. Physical affection in marriage is very important to me.

\_\_\_24. I love it when someone wants to spend time with me alone.

\_\_\_25. I feel blessed when someone notices what I do and says, "Good job!"

\_\_\_26. It is meaningful to me to be held and cared for after a hard day.

\_\_\_27. Even when I am confident about my talents and gifts, I welcome input and help from others.

\_\_\_28. When I feel stressed out or down, sympathy and encouragement from other people are very meaningful to me.

\_\_\_29. I feel good when someone expresses satisfaction with the way I am.

\_\_\_30. I enjoy being in a group of people when they are talking positively about me.

\_\_\_31. I would describe myself as a touchy-feely person.

\_\_\_32. It is important that my input is considered in a decision that will affect my life or schedule.

\_\_\_33. I feel blessed when someone shows interest in the projects I am working on.

\_\_\_34. I like trophies, plaques, and special gifts that commemorate something significant I have done.

\_\_\_35. I sometimes worry about the future.

\_\_\_36. When in a new environment, I immediately search for a group of people to connect with.

___37. The thought of moving, starting a new job or class, or making other changes fills me with anxiety.

___38. It bothers me when people are prejudiced against others because they dress or act differently.

___39. I need to be surrounded by friends and loved ones who will be there through thick and thin.

___40. I feel blessed when someone thanks me for something I have done.

___41. It is very meaningful to me to know that someone is praying for me.

___42. I am bothered by people who try to control others.

___43. I feel blessed when I receive undeserved and spontaneous expressions of love.

___44. I am pleased when someone looks me in the eyes and really listens when I talk.

___45. I feel blessed when people commend me for any godly characteristic I exhibit.

___46. It is important to me to have a soul mate stand with me when I am hurting or in trouble.

___47. I don't enjoy working alone. I would rather have someone working with me.

___48. It is important to me to feel as if I am a part of the group.

___49. I respond positively when someone seeks to understand my emotions and shows me loving concern.

___50. When working on a project, I would much rather work with a team of people than by myself.

# Identifying Your Top Needs

INSTRUCTIONS
Using the numbers
(-2, -1, 0, +1, +2) you
placed in the blank in
front of each item in
the Intimacy Needs
Assessment
Inventory, add up the
numbers to discover
what your total is for
each of the ten
intimacy needs:

1. Add up your
responses to
statements:
1_____
19_____
36_____
38_____
48_____
Total_____
These responses
relate to the need for
ACCEPTANCE.

2. Add up your
responses to
statements:
2_____
17_____
35_____
37_____
39_____
Total _____
These responses
relate to the need for
SECURITY.

3. Add up your
responses to
statements:
11_____
18_____
25_____
34_____
40_____
Total _____
These responses
relate to the need for
APPRECIATION.

4. Add up your
responses to
statements:
3_____
15_____
21_____
33_____
41_____
Total _____
These responses
relate to the need for
ENCOURAGEMENT.

5. Add up your responses to statements:

4_____

14_____

22_____

32_____

42_____

Total _____

These responses relate to the need for RESPECT.

6. Add up your responses to statements:

5 _____

13_____

23_____

31_____

43_____

Total _____

These responses relate to the need for AFFECTION.

7. Add up your responses to statements:

6 _____

12_____

24_____

30_____

44_____

Total _____

These responses relate to the need for ATTENTION.

8. Add up your responses to statements:

7 _____

16_____

20_____

29_____

45_____

Total _____

These responses relate to the need for APPROVAL.

9. Add up your responses to statements:

10_____

26_____

28_____

46_____

49_____

Total _____

These responses relate to the need for COMFORT.

10. Add up your responses to statements:

8 _____

9 _____

27_____

47 _____

50_____

Total _____

These responses relate to the need for SUPPORT.

## REFLECTIONS

1. What were your three highest totals? Which needs do they represent?

_____

_____

_____

2. What were your three lowest totals? Which needs do they represent?

_____

_____

_____

3. What were your spouse's highest and lowest totals?

_____

_____

_____

# APPENDIX B

# About Intimate Life Ministries

## Who and What Is Intimate Life Ministries?

Intimate Life Ministries (ILM) is a training and resource ministry, headquartered in Austin, Texas, whose purpose is *to assist in the development of Great Commandment ministries worldwide,* ongoing ministries that deepen our intimacy with God and with others in marriage, family, and the church.

Intimate Life Ministries comprises:

- A network of **churches** seeking to fortify homes and communities with his love;
- A network of **pastors and other ministry leaders** walking intimately with God and their families and seeking to live vulnerably before their people;
- A team of **accredited trainers** committed to helping churches establish ongoing Great Commandment ministries;
- A team of **professional associates** from ministry and other professional Christian backgrounds, assisting with research, training, and resource development;
- **Christian broadcasters,** publishers, media, and other affiliates, cooperating to see marriages and families reclaimed as divine relationships;
- **Headquarters staff** providing strategic planning, coordination, and support.

## How Can Intimate Life Ministries Serve You?

ILM's Great Commandment Network of Churches is an effective ongoing support and equipping relationship with churches and Christian leaders. There are at least four ways ILM can serve you:

## 1. MINISTERING TO MINISTRY LEADERS

ILM offers a unique two-day "Galatians 6:6" retreat to ministers and their spouses for personal renewal and to reestablish and affirm ministry and family priorities. The conference accommodations and meals are provided as a gift to ministry leaders by cosponsoring partners. Thirty to forty such retreats are held throughout the U.S., Europe, and other locations each year.

## 2. PARTNERING WITH DENOMINATIONS AND OTHER MINISTRIES

Numerous denominations and ministries have partnered with ILM by "commissioning" us to equip their ministry leaders through the Galatians 6:6 retreats along with strategic training and ongoing resources. This unique partnership enables a denomination to use the expertise of ILM trainers and resources to perpetuate a movement of Great Commandment ministry at the local level. ILM also provides a crisis-support setting where denominations may send ministers, couples, or families who are struggling in their relationships.

## 3. IDENTIFYING, TRAINING, AND EQUIPPING LAY LEADERS

ILM is committed to helping the church equip its lay leaders through:

- *Sermon Series* on several Great Commandment topics to help pastors communicate a vision for Great Commandment health as well as identify and cultivate a core lay leadership group.
- *Community Training Classes* that provide weekly or weekend training to church staff and lay leaders. Classes are delivered by Intimate Life trainers along with ILM video-assisted training, workbooks, study courses, etc.
- *One-Day Training Conferences* on implementing Great Commandment ministry in the local church through marriage, parenting, or singles ministry. Conducted by Intimate Life trainers, these conferences are a great way to jump-start Great Commandment ministry in a local church.

## 4. PROVIDING ADVANCED TRAINING AND CRISIS SUPPORT

ILM conducts advanced training for both ministry staff and lay leaders through the Leadership Institute, focusing on relational ministry (marriage, parenting, families, singles, men, women, blended families, counseling, etc.). The Enrichment Center provides support to relationships in crisis through Intensive Retreats for couples, families, and singles.

For more information on how you, your church, or your denomination can take advantage of the many services offered by Intimate Life Ministries, write or call:

Intimate Life Ministries
P.O. Box 201808
Austin, TX 78720-1808
1-800-881-8008

Or visit our Web site at www.ilministries.org

# About the Authors

**David and Teresa Ferguson,** married for more than thirty-five years, are the directors of Intimate Life Ministries, which serves thousands of churches and ministry leaders worldwide with a message of how to deepen intimacy with God and deepen relationships in marriage, family, and the church.

Early in David's ministry, he, like so many other people in Christian ministry, tried unsuccessfully to achieve balance between ministry and family demands. Out of an intense desire to honor God and minister to the needs of his family, he rediscovered a biblical principle that transformed his life, his family, and his ministry to others. He writes about that journey in his book *The Great Commandment Principle*. For the past twenty years David and Teresa have been sharing that message in print and through ministry retreats, media, and speaking engagements around the world.

David's graduate work in theology, counseling, and social sciences focused on the Great Commandment principle and its impact on relationships, ministry, and culture. David has earned a M.Ed. from Southwest Texas State University as well as a Ph.D. and a Litt.D. from Oxford Graduate School. He is a member of the Oxford Society of Scholars.

David and Teresa have collaborated on the writing of several books and articles. They live in Austin, Texas, and have three adult children—Terri, Robin, and Eric.